HELP! *My Friend's In Trouble!*

HELP! *My Friend's In Trouble!*

Supporting Your Friends Who Struggle With ...

- *Family Problems*
- *Sexual Crises*
- *Food Addictions*
- *Self-Esteem*
- *Depression, Grief and Loss*

Susie Shellenberger

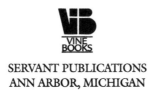

SERVANT PUBLICATIONS
ANN ARBOR, MICHIGAN

Vine Books is an imprint of Servant Publications especially designed to serve
evangelical Christians.

Published in association with the literary agency of Alive Communications, Inc.,
1465 Kelly Johnson Blvd., Suite 320, Colorado Springs, CO 80920.

Published by Servant Publications
P.O. Box 8617
Ann Arbor, Michigan 48107

Cover design: Left Coast Design, Portland, Oregon
Cover photograph: © Color Day Productions/The Image Bank

00 01 02 03 10 9 8 7 6 5 4 3 2 1

Printed in the United States of America
ISBN 1-56955-165-0

Cataloging-in-Publication Data on file at the Library of Congress.

read this first ...

... to find out how this book works. You already know that this is a book about helping your friends with their problems. But to *help* your friend, you've gotta *be* a friend. And ... well, you've gotta *have* friends.

So Section One deals with some good ol' basic fun stuff on making and keeping friends.

Section Two deals at length with some heavy issues that some of your friends may be battling.

Section Three is a collection of several problems you *and* your friends may be having.

Hey, before you begin reading this book, I first want to congratulate you on even *having* it. I mean, just the fact that you're *holding* this book tells me you really care about your friends. That's awesome!

"But Susie, I'm just one person. Can I really make a difference in my friend's life?"

You bet you can! All through history, "ones" have been making a huge difference. For instance, did you know:

- Just *one* vote caused King Charles I of England to be beheaded in 1649.

- *One* vote made Adolph Hitler head of the Nazi Party in 1923.

- Just *one* vote determined that Americans would speak English rather than German in 1776.
- In 1845, *one* vote brought Texas into the Union.
- In 1868, *one* vote saved President Andrew Johnson from impeachment.
- *One* vote elected Thomas Jefferson president in 1800.
- Just *one* man, Noah, heard and obeyed God's voice. The ark he built saved the entire animal kingdom and procreated humankind.
- She was just one woman—and single, too!—but Phoebe volunteered to deliver Paul's letter to the Romans. And how that book has influenced millions of Christians through the ages!
- Just *one* man—the Son of God, the greatest gift of all—offers eternal life to you and me ... and to your friends who are battling deep hurt.

You bet you can make a difference in your friend's life! ONE is extremely powerful—especially when Jesus Christ is the One doing the empowering!

God bless you as you seek to be Jesus to those around you.

dedication

For Kathy Gowler

It was in a tiny, primitive village in the middle of the jungle at the end of the world on one of our adventure treks that we learned the Kirikiri Tribe had a special word for friend—**oolie:** *one who carries me.*

I think there was actually another syllable to the word, but that's as much as we could understand. And it has stuck. You truly *are* an oolie. We have carried each other around the world, cuddled orphans in Romania, jet-skied on the Indian Ocean, safaried in Africa, snorkeled Australia's Great Barrier Reef, nearly broke an escalator in Singapore and laughed till our sides hurt.

Since this book is about friendship, I can't help but think of you as I fill these pages. I only wish everyone the whole world over could understand that friendship smothered in Jesus Christ produces oolieness—*friends who carry one another*—through midnight tears, lost files and a multitude of prayers to our Father.

Thank you, Friend. My Sisto. My Oolie.

contents

ON *Being, Making and Keeping a Friend*

Real friends are those who, when you've made a fool of yourself, don't feel that you've done a permanent job.

Author unknown

Six No-Fail Secrets
for Making Friends

Jamie always had a crowd around her. She wasn't especially knock-out gorgeous. She usually had a couple of zits, and she wasn't exceptionally good at sports. But she was one of the most popular students at school. Everyone loved her!

Jamie was a friend magnet. Wherever she went, someone wanted to be with her. It wasn't unusual for Jamie to be seen listening to one of the football players share a problem or showing a new student how to get to the biology lab.

Why? What was it about Jamie that made everyone notice her? If her looks and her talents weren't anything to brag about, what *did* she have going for her?

Here it is, short and simple: Jamie had learned the six secrets for making and keeping friends.

You already know this book is about helping your friends who are struggling with hurt, confusion and a variety of problems. But guess what? In order for you to be a helping friend, you first have to *have* friends and be the kind of friend others *want* in their lives.

So before we actually get into how you can *help* your friends, let's first take a peek at how you *get* friends and *become* a friend, OK? (If you don't feel you need this part, just skim it quickly before you flip to the next section, which starts on page 35.) Otherwise, let's take a look at the first secret!

Friend-Making Secret #1:
Be Nice to Everyone!

Wait a sec, you're thinking. *That's too easy. There's gotta be more to friendship than that!*

Yeah, there are a few more strategies we'll talk about in a few seconds, but the biggest secret of all—the one thousands of teens try to skip over—is simply being nice to *everyone*.

Jamie was as kind to the new student who had no friends at all as she was to the football player. She had friends in the band and friends in drama. She refused to associate with only one group of people. Because she was kind to everyone, people responded by wanting to be around her.

> Dear friends, **let us love one another,** for love comes from God.
>
> 1 JOHN 4:7, emphasis mine

OK, now that you know the first secret, are you ready for the others? Let's move on....

Friend-Making Secret #2:
Cultivate a Sensational Smile!

There's something intriguing about someone who smiles a lot, isn't there? We're automatically drawn to someone who's happy. And a smile usually makes the person behind it seem approachable.

If people know you're approachable, they'll start coming to *you.* And how will they know? Well, you'll make them feel at ease and comfortable. And how does *that* happen? By smiling. A smile is an open invitation to be approached. It says, "You can talk to me. I'll be friendly with you. Really. It's OK. I'm not going to hurt you."

Smiles also convey something else that's really important when making friends. A smiling person suggests confidence. (That was really a great point, did you get it? Or did you just zoom by it quickly? Well, to make sure you get it, let's go over it again, OK?)

Repeat after me: **Smiling suggests confidence.**

"But Susie, I'm NOT confident. I feel insecure, and I'm always worried about what I look like and what everyone else is thinking, and ..."

Whoa. Go grab some lemonade from the fridge and cool off. I said *suggests* not *proves.* You don't have to actually *feel* confident to smile. But when you *do,* people will *think* you're confident. Cool, huh? (Watch the lemonade. You're starting to drip.)

But here's something even cooler: The longer you practice smiling—even in intimidating situations—the sooner your smile will catch up with you. In other words, you'll start to believe what the smile stands for. You'll gain confidence from smiling! No, it won't happen overnight, but it *will* happen. I promise.

Let me introduce you to sixteen-year-old Jenny. I met Jenny

along with three hundred other teen girls I took to Brazil with me on a two-week missions trip. On the final night of the trip, several girls stepped up to the microphone and shared what God had taught them during the past few days.

I'll never forget Jenny. Smiling from ear to ear, she shared her story. "When I was eleven," she began, "I was in a terrible car accident. My bottom teeth were knocked out—causing my mouth to be disfigured. I struggled a *lot* with having low self-esteem, thinking I was ugly. But you know what? God has shown me that I have a beautiful smile! And my smile is something I can give to everyone I meet. Because he can use my smile to minister to others and to encourage those around me, I no longer have to worry about my outer appearance. God is using my smile!"

Wow. Jenny had learned the secret of flashing a sensational smile. And she was right! God *was* using her smile. Jenny always had a crowd of people around her. She was approachable, easy to talk to, and she genuinely cared about others. Know what else? She was beginning to *feel* the confidence that her smile *suggested!*

What about you? Will you make a point to start working right now on developing a sensational smile? Just for fun (since you've already dripped lemonade all over this page anyway) I'll leave some space here for you to doodle on. Know what I want you to doodle? Smiles. Make as many as you want. Big ones. Little ones. Funny ones. Magnetic ones. Create a million smiles right here, and I'll go grab a Cherry 7-Up and meet you on the next page with "friend-making secret #3!"

Friend-Making Secret #3:
Learn How to Talk **and** Listen to Other People

It wasn't unusual at all to see Jamie listening to someone sharing a problem, but she was also a good conversationalist. In other words, the other person didn't have to do all the talking.

Everyone knows someone who talks all the time. They're not much fun to be around, are they? I once had a friend with whom I went out to eat a lot. She talked all the time. As in nonstop. Once in a while, she'd say, "Susie, I don't understand you. You travel all over the place and speak to thousands of teenagers every year, but you sure don't say much one-on-one."

I *wanted* to say, "How can I? You never give me a chance!"

Everyone wants to talk. We all have a story to tell. Each of us enjoy having someone listen to what we say. It makes us feel important when someone is truly interested in what we're saying.

Learn to listen. When other people find out you're willing to listen, believe me, they'll talk—and they'll be talking to *you!* But when you listen … *really* listen. I'm talking about genuine listening—not the kind of "listening" where you focus your eyes on the person speaking, but your mind is focused on the cute guy who's approaching your table.

When someone is talking to you, zero in 100 percent on *that person*. It's easy to tell when someone's just pretending to listen but really thinking about something else. That won't fly in making friends. You'll be known as a phony.

"OK, but once I've learned to be a great listener, what am I going to do with all the stuff I'm hearing? Sometimes I feel like I just gotta tell someone!"

Oooh. That's a good one.

You're going to have to learn to keep secrets. That's part of being a good listener. A genuine friend is one who can be trusted. When Josh tells you in confidence that he likes Bethany, you can't run off and tell her—even though you think you're just gonna die if you don't. Remember ...

A **gossip** separates close friends.

PROVERBS 16:28

"Is it ever right to break a secret?"

Another good question. And the answer is yes. If your friend is in danger of hurting herself or someone else, you can't keep that information private. But we'll talk more about that later when we get into how to help your friends who are going through really rough times.

Back to keeping secrets. Make it a priority. When people realize they can trust you—truly trust you—they'll feel safe in opening up to you with their problems, hurts, questions, fears and dreams.

Talking tips. Listening is only half of becoming a great conversationalist. It's just as important to *talk* as it is to listen. The key is learning *when* to talk.

Try not to talk just to hear yourself talking. That brings us back to my friend who just talked and talked and talked all-l-l-l-l the time. No one else gets a word in edgewise. On the other hand, don't put the burden of the entire conversation on someone else. You've got to do your part, too.

"But why do I have to learn to talk to guys? Isn't it better just to let them talk about themselves?"

Well, let's find out what the guys really think. Seventeen-year-old Lance says, "It always freaks me out when I'm with a girl who expects me to do all the talking. That's too much pressure. I like being with girls who can hold their own end of the conversation."

Jeremy feels the same way: "Sometimes I'll be with a girl who acts like she's afraid to say something. I mean, how else are we gonna get to know each other if we don't talk and listen? But sometimes girls act like what they have to say isn't important. Of course it is! I wouldn't be spending time with a girl, trying to carry on a conversation with her, if I didn't care about what she has to say."

Guess what? Lance and Jeremy aren't the only ones who feel this way. Everyone wants to be in a friendship that has both give and take when it comes to talking.

"Yeah, but what if I just don't know what to say?"

I hear you. And I understand. Here's a little secret: If you're really listening to what the other person is saying, you can ask questions about what he's talking about.

Eric just mentioned he has a lot of math homework. So make a question out of what you've heard: "Do you like math?"

"Ah, it's OK. But Mrs. Johnson sure gives us a lot of homework!"

Now grab your next question from what he's just told you.

"I haven't had Mrs. Johnson. Is she a good teacher? Does she explain things well?"

Of course, you don't always have to continue the conversation by asking questions. Throw your own thoughts out there as well. Again, Eric has just mentioned he has a lot of math homework. You contribute your own thoughts: "I don't have any math homework, but I've got a huge report to write on this play called *Our Town* that we've been reading in Lit."

"Yeah, OK. But Eric and I already know each other. How do I get a conversation going with someone I don't know at all, or someone I know—but not really well?"

Asking questions is the best way to get a conversation going. Even if you know the person really well and you're already good friends, asking questions will help you get to know them even better.

About a year ago, I went on a safari in Kenya, Africa, with a friend of mine. Knowing it was going to be a lo-o-o-o-n-n-n-g flight from Colorado Springs to Nairobi, Kenya, I took one of my favorite books along: *The Book of Questions.*

Even though we were already great friends (after all, we were traveling across the world together!), we still had a blast asking fun questions and learning more about each other from our answers.

Since I love questions so much, I decided to create a list of my own to use when the need arises. I'll share them with you, and you can try them out on friends, acquaintances and even people you don't know yet. I'll give you twenty questions, and I'll leave some space for you to create five of your own to add to the list, OK? Here goes:

Twenty Questions to Talk About

1. If you had to give up one of your five senses (sight, hearing, taste, touch, smell), which would you choose to live without?
2. If you suddenly won a million dollars, how would you spend it?
3. If you could receive truthful answers to any two questions, *what* would you ask and to *whom* would you ask it?
4. Is it always wrong to kill? What about insects? Animals?
5. If you could be a contestant on any TV game show, which would you choose?
6. Would you be willing to have super-frightening dreams every night for three years if it meant you'd be really popular the rest of your life?
7. Do you think there's life on other planets?

8. If *you* were Eve, would *you* have eaten the forbidden fruit? (Or, if *you* were Adam, would *you* have blamed it on *Eve?*)

9. If you could invent a brand-new chewing gum, what would you call it? How would it differ from all other gum on the market? What flavor would it be?

10. What's the most frightening thing that's ever happened to you so far?

11. What's the most valuable thing you own?

12. What's one thing your parents were right about after all?

13. What makes you laugh uncontrollably?

14. If you had to choose between TV and radio, which would you do without for an entire year?

15. What's the difference between encouraging someone and complimenting someone?

16. If you could write a book, what would you title it? What would it be about?

17. What's the most recent book you've read?

18. What classes in school do you think will be completely useless to you in the future?

19. If you could live anywhere in the world for one year, where would it be?

20. What's the most exciting thing going on in your life *right now*?

OK, it's your turn! Think of five more questions and jot them here in the space provided. Then let's move on to Secret #4!

1. _____

2. _____

3. _____

4. _____

5. _____

Friend-Making Secret #4:
Don't Be a Know-It-All!

Heather always had a better story. Whenever someone talked about their family vacation, Heather piped up with a better vacation. And when someone told a joke, Heather always tried to outdo it with a funnier joke.

When someone asked Heather a question, she'd always give them an answer—even when she didn't know the answer! It wasn't long before people stopped asking for her opinion about things. They got tired of being around her. She was a know-it-all.

Why do people like Heather act that way? Why are they always trying to outdo someone else's story or make others think they know it all?

Insecurity. Insecurity. Insecurity.

Either you really *do* know a lot and just like to show off so you can be the center of attention (which means you're insecure), or you really *don't* know it all, but you want people to *think* you do, because you're afraid if they think you *don't* know everything, they won't like you (which means you're insecure).

Guess what? You don't have to be the center of attention! It's really OK to blend in. You don't always have to be the star—the one who's right, the one who has the best story.

Nor do you always have to have the answer. If people befriend you simply because of your knowledge, they're not real friends anyway. If you have a friend who falls into this know-it-all category, you can help her climb out by letting her know that she doesn't have to earn your friendship.

If *you're* the one in the know-it-all division, allow God to help you move from the spotlight of attention to focusing on the needs of others. Humility is extremely attractive. Ask God to help you become humble.

In fact, why wait? Let's pray about it right now.

Dear Jesus,

I confess I've done some not-so-nice things to be the center of attention. I've interrupted. I've made up stories. I've talked loud. I've bragged about stuff.

Will you forgive me, Father? I don't want to be insecure and always fighting for attention. I want to be like you— humble yet confident; interested in others yet willing to share myself with people.

Teach me how to be humble, Jesus. Thank you.

In your name I pray, Amen.

Want to stay on the right track? Here's a terrific Scripture verse to memorize:

Do not think of yourself more highly than you ought, but rather think of yourself with sober judgment, in accordance with the measure of faith God has given you.

ROMANS 12:3

Friend-Making Secret #5:
Be Yourself!

Tawni was really frustrated! Hannah's dad was totally rich, and almost every week Hannah arrived at school wearing super-expensive stuff, like jeans that cost $100 or a jacket for $350 or new shoes that were easily $200.

Tawni couldn't keep up. Even though most of the girls tried to imitate what Hannah did and wore, Tawni had had enough. Instead of being a follower, she finally decided to simply be herself. To set her own trends. To stop focusing on what others were doing.

So one Saturday, she and her mom went thrift-store shopping. Tawni had only $20 saved from baby-sitting, but as it turned out, that was all she needed! She got a whole stash of great stuff.

When they got home, her mom helped her customize her new clothes just for her. They cut the jeans into below-the-knee capri style, and sewed funky patches on both legs.

They mixed and matched a few of her other purchases, and they created a totally-cool hat out of something no one would have guessed had any more life to it. Tawni got a weird-looking pair of shoes for $2—which was great, because she liked weird stuff. With the help of her mom, Tawni put together a brand-new outfit.

Yeah, people looked at her on Monday morning when she walked into school. Especially Hannah. "Tawni! I love it! I've got to have it. Please take me shopping with you next week!"

You guessed it. It wasn't long before thrift-store shopping became the "in" thing to do. By deciding to simply be herself, Tawni had become a trendsetter.

What about you? Are you being *you*, or are you simply trying to imitate everyone else? God created you in his image. He has made you unique and special. He doesn't want you copycatting those around you. He wants you to be *you*—the way he created you.

"But, Susie. What if instead of starting a trend, being myself makes people laugh at me? I'd be so embarrassed!"

Never imitate others simply because you're afraid to be yourself. Check *this* out:

Fear not, for I have redeemed you; I have called you by name; you are mine.

ISAIAH 43:1

That's terrific ammunition for eliminating fear and self-consciousness. If God himself chooses us, redeems us and calls us by our name, what do we have to fear? When we truly realize that the King of Kings accepts us and loves us just as we are, that sets us free from having to impress others, imitate others or follow others.

Still with me? Good. Time for the last secret! And ... drum-roll, please ...

Friend-Making Secret #6:
Add Value to Those Around You!

Carrie, like Jamie, always has a crowd of people around her. She's twenty-one now, but since she was in junior high, she's always been one of the most popular students in school. Now, as she's completing her college education, once again, she's one of the most popular people on campus.

I pulled Carrie aside and asked what her secret was: "I have a list of twenty things I try to do every day," she said. "There are some things on the list that change and fluctuate, but there are a few things that remain the same."

"Give me an example of something that remains the same—something you try to do every single day," I said.

"OK. Well, I try really hard to add value to those around me."

"Every day?" I questioned.

"Every day," she said. "People light up when you recognize something they do well and let them know it. It only takes a minute to give someone a compliment or to notice what gifts a person has. So why not bring attention to it? It automatically adds value to how they see themselves. I want to be the kind of person that's always seeing the positive attributes in others. I don't ever want to tear someone down. When Jesus walked the earth, he affirmed and encouraged. I want to do that, too. I want to build people up."

I decided to hang out with her a couple of weeks and watch her in action. It was true! Carrie *daily* brought worth to those around her by noticing the good in their lives. "A generous man will prosper; he who refreshes others will himself be refreshed" (Proverbs 11:25).

She complimented our bus driver. She sat with a teen girl who was confused about her boyfriend, and Carrie affirmed the girl's willingness to obey God—even if it meant breaking up with the guy.

Carrie told Brett she saw a real depth about him. She told Matt it was cool to see him using his musical gifts to glorify the Lord. She noticed that Nikki was not only great with large groups of people but that she was also terrific one-on-one, and Carrie let Nikki know. The list goes on and on. Genuinely, Carrie affirms those around her adding value to their lives.

Will you determine to do the same? Find something good in each of your family members and encourage them with it. Look for people who go the extra mile for others, and tell them you notice. Watch those who are shy and highlight their tender spirits. You'll find it's amazing to see people actually light up when you affirm them and add value to what they're already doing well!

Time to Recap

Following those six strategies really *will* help you make friends. Let's recap one more time—I want to make sure you don't forget!

Popularity is gained through:
1. Being nice to everyone.
2. Cultivating a sensational smile.
3. Knowing how to talk *and* listen.
4. Not being a know-it-all.
5. Being yourself.
6. Adding value to those around you.

But wait! There's more! Even though those six secrets will help you develop good friendships, there's still something reallyreallyreally important I've gotta tell you.

Before I tell you what it is, I need to be honest with you: This last item may not help you make friends. In fact, you might even *lose* a few. But it is THE most important thing you'll ever do in your life.

The Most Important Secret of All:
Be Jesus to Those Around You!

Since Jesus isn't here in the flesh, he's depending on us to be his hands, feet, arms, ears. Are you using your hands, feet, arms and ears to bring glory to him? What about the rest of you? Are your eyes seeing people as Jesus sees them? Does your mouth speak words of encouragement as Jesus would? Is your voice singing praises to his name?

Are you going the extra mile for someone who needs you? (That's what the rest of this book is about, so we need to get this part settled right now.) *Jesus always loved.* He calls you to do the same.

When your friends are hurting, love them.

When Juli battles an eating disorder, love her.

When Brooke shares that she's been abused, love her.

When Geoff confides that his parents are splitting, be Jesus to him.

If Austin tells you that his mother is dying of cancer, he doesn't need a bunch of philosophical words from you. He needs you to reflect the love of Jesus to him.

"Does being Jesus to my friends mean not judging them when they do stuff they shouldn't?"

Sometimes Jesus loved with "tough love." In other words, he never made excuses for people's sin. He never said, "Well, that's OK. You didn't mean to." He allowed people to feel guilty for the disobedience in their lives, but he continued to love them.

You do the same. And when your friends are lashing out, either in rebellion or because of deep hurts, don't allow them to make excuses. Love them like Jesus would. Sometimes that means giving a hug. Sometimes it means telling them something they don't want to hear, like: "I'll be here for you, but you've got to go ask him to forgive you." Or "You really need to see a counselor but I'll go with you."

Being Jesus to your friends may not be easy, because Jesus didn't always do the popular thing—he always did the *right* thing. And sometimes doing what's right may cost you some friends.

Being Jesus means being willing to be a servant. Jesus told his disciples to serve—wash each other's feet. And to set the example, he knelt before them and washed *their* feet. Imagine! The Creator of the universe washing feet! (See John 13:1-17 for the whole story.)

Be imitators of God.

EPHESIANS 5:1

Washing feet can get stinky. It's uncomfortable. It's not easy. But it's right.

I had taken a group of teens on a missions trip to South America. During the middle of the trip, I gave a devotion on how Jesus has called us to be servants. I called someone up front, knelt in front of him and washed his feet. Then we divided into small groups and began to wash each other's feet.

One group left the room and went outside for more privacy. As they were washing each other's feet, a national military man walked by. On an impulse, Jarod politely stopped him and motioned for the officer to sit on the ground with them.

A couple of teens from the group gently untied the man's shoes. One of the girls picked up his feet and placed them in the basin of water. Jarod began washing. Calvin grabbed the towel and tenderly dried the officer's feet.

One by one, they began sharing the difference Christ had made in their lives. When they had finished, the military officer was asking how he could know Jesus like they did. He prayed and surrendered his life to Jesus.

Why? Because a great evangelist had come to town? No. Because of a dazzling Christian concert with flashing lights and smoke machines? No. Simply because a group of teens were determined to reach out and be Jesus to him.

God isn't asking you to be flashy. He may or may not provide you with a stage or a microphone. But he *is* calling you to serve. To reach out. To be his hands to those around you. To be him to a lost and dying world.

Will you do it? Even when it's tough? When you're wanting to help your friends come out on top of their problems, the very *best* thing you can do is to be Jesus to them.

Let us not love with words or tongue but with **actions** and in **truth.**

1 JOHN 3:18, emphasis mine

* * *

And now we're getting down to why you are reading this book—you *do* want to help your friends. They're hurting. Some of them are struggling with a heaviness that's almost beyond description. Let's help them, OK? Being Jesus to them will have eternal effects! Turn the page. It's time to start.

"HELP! My Friend ..."

Greater love has no one than this, that one
lay down his life for his *friends.*

JOHN 15:13

TWO

Help!
My Friend Has an Eating Disorder!

Laura's dieting had become much more than *important*. It had grown into a full-fledged *obsession*. I asked her to share her story with you so that you can understand a little better what may be going through the mind of a friend who's struggling with an eating disorder.

Fighting the Food Phantom
by Laura Johnson, R.D./L.D.
as told to Tracy Pullen, R.D./L.D.

Why?
Why did I scarf all that stuff?
A medium pizza, three doughnuts, two large bowls of ice cream,
Chinese food, four pieces of cinnamon toast....
What made me do it?
Now it's all in my stomach ... bloating my body like a balloon.
I've got to get rid of it.
I'll make myself throw up. Then I'll take some strong laxatives.
One more time I'll rid myself of everything inside.
Tomorrow WILL be a new day.
Surely, after THIS binge, my nightmare will stop....
Or will it?

I was the victim of a deadly eating disorder known as bulimia. For ten years it raged out of control in my life like a flaming inferno—sending me on frequent eating rampages.

I'd swallow everything I could get my hands on. Then, when my belly was painfully swollen, I'd make my way to the nearest rest room.

My horrible bulimic nightmare began during my sophomore year of high school. But the roots stemmed much deeper ... way back to junior high and my struggles with a tough home life and a poor self-image.

I felt so awkward and ugly back then. My tall frame was undeveloped, and my straight red hair hung limply across my shoulders.

Why didn't I have any friends? Was it because I wore no makeup? I felt like the campus alien with my fair-skinned complexion. All the other kids were trim, tan and trendy. They wore sharp clothes and had all the flashy accessories to go with the latest styles.

Surface Solution

When high school rolled around, I'd finally had enough. I got so tired of feeling like an outcast that I vowed to make a complete change during Christmas break of my sophomore year. I got my hair cut and styled, had my "colors" done, started using makeup and hit the campus a new woman.

"Laura—is that YOU?" my girlfriends exclaimed.

"WOW ... where have you been all our lives?" guys would ask. (The same ones who never gave me the time of day before.)

It suddenly felt good to have people notice me—especially the boys! I loved all the attention, and knew I was actually a very attractive young lady.

I also increased my school activities and determined to become more involved. I joined the band, played basketball, softball and competed on the track team.

Mom was thrilled that I was finally coming out of my shell. Especially since things were so messed up at home.

Torn on the Inside

Dad was an alcoholic, impossible to live with at times. Whenever stuff bugged him, he'd turn to a bottle for relief. Then he'd take his anger out on us. I was sick of tiptoeing around on egg shells … but Mom insisted we keep a tight lip about our family secret.

Eventually, she started living out her life through me. I guess Mom wanted her daughter to experience some of the things she missed in life. So she pushed me to excel.

"Whatever you do, give it your absolute best," she'd tell me. So I pasted a smile on my face and vowed to work harder at everything—popularity, high grades, achieving a stunning appearance. If my performance wasn't perfect, it wasn't acceptable.

But this double life was draining. Pushing myself to be perfect in public, then facing the pain at home tore me up inside. Especially seeing my dad drunk—and my mom crushed.

"We can't go on like this," I'd tell Mom. "Dad needs help!"

"This is a *private* family matter," Mom would say.

My lips were sealed, but my heart ached.

The Secret to Slender?

Despite the hard times at home, things really seemed to click at school.

Toward the end of my junior year, I was thrilled to learn

that the faculty and administration had selected *me* to represent our student body at a prestigious and fun leadership conference. Girls from all over the state of Oklahoma would be attending, and I'd have a chance not only to make new friends but to develop leadership skills as well.

Attending Girls State seemed like a lifesaver. It meant time away from home and less pressure. Most of all, there was no fear of running into a drunken parent.

During the week, however, I couldn't help noticing how much my roommates were eating. They were chowing down on all my faves—hot fudge sundaes, pizza, chips, cookies … yet they all had fabulous figures. Toward the end of our stay, a girl named Nancy filled me in on their secret.

"We can eat anything we want. It's easy, Laura. After you're finished just go to the bathroom and make yourself throw up."

The idea repulsed me at first, but I so desperately wanted to maintain a good figure—and the thought of never having to skip a meal again to lose weight sounded great. I accepted her suggestion.

Forcing my finger down my throat seemed weird, but after I threw up the first time, I thought, *Hey, this isn't so bad. And it actually works!*

I did it a second time, then a third. Before I knew it, I was purging my food on a regular basis. But that was only the beginning.

The Raging Battle

In time, I learned what foods I could eat a lot of and throw up easily. Ice cream was one of them, so I consumed large quantities of the creamy sweet stuff. Soon, I started taking several laxatives every day—along with throwing up—to hasten the process.

Weeks merged into years and my once-simple key to a knock-out bod turned into an out-of-control obsession. I found myself waking daily to the same haunting question: *Will I be able to eat normally today without throwing up? Can I make it one day without laxatives or diet pills?*

But the inferno raged within. It became difficult to sit through English and concentrate on adjectives and adverbs when I was mentally creating an intricate plan of when I would binge and purge next. I spent more than $25 a day on food, consuming between 7,000 and 10,000 calories.

Bruised by Bulimia

Little did I know that the inside of my body was slowly deteriorating. I knew what I was doing wasn't normal, but at least I had a flat stomach.

Eventually, throwing up everything I ate made me feel terrible about myself, despite my figure. I got to the point where I really *wanted* to stop ... but couldn't.

I felt as though I was on a high-speed roller coaster and couldn't get off. I wanted to stop the ride, but I knew I'd have to do it myself. The thought of others finding out that I had this big problem—and that I wasn't perfect—literally *terrified* me.

I began my own private search for a cure. I attended seminars on eating disorders, read books, studied nutrition and eventually became a registered dietitian.

If I can just learn all the proper information about food and place myself on the right diet, I told myself, *I'll be able to eat normally and the nightmare will be over.*

It didn't work. As a professional nutritionist, I easily put others on diets but couldn't make one work for myself. I felt like I had fallen into a deep, black hole and couldn't climb out. No light. No hope. No answers.

Steps to Recovery

Then *he* came along. Bryce ... the man of my dreams. He seemed too good to be true. He was everything I ever dreamed about in a boyfriend ... tall, blond, handsome, sensitive.

Bryce and I fell in love. And as our relationship grew, I knew he was the man I wanted to spend the rest of my life with. For the first time ever, I met someone who seemed to love me unconditionally.

But would he still love me if he knew about my secret? I often wondered as he wrapped his strong arms around me.

We just couldn't get engaged until I told him about my horrible nightmare. At the same time, though, I didn't want him to know.

In desperation, I went to a counselor named Dr. Morris.

"Doctor, I've been bulimic for ten years," I told him as I entered his office. "I need help. I can't go on like this."

He rubbed his chin and smiled warmly. "Laura, I'm glad you've come to me. You're facing a problem that can't be handled alone.

"I have a group of people with eating disorders that I meet with weekly for intensive counseling," he continued. "I'd like you to be a part of the group."

My eyes opened wide and a pain shot through my stomach. "No!" I rebelled. "No way, Doctor. I don't want anyone else to know about my problem. Can't the two of us just work it out?"

Dr. Morris reminded me that my bulimia had been a private matter for such a long time that I *needed* to verbalize with others who were going through the same thing.

I had no other option, and things just had to change ... so I agreed.

I thought I'd feel some ray of hope when I finally took this dreaded step, but the doctor threw me a *real* curve ball.

"Laura, Bryce needs to know," he said. "I cannot let you join the group until you tell him what's going on."

"That's not fair!" I screamed. "I want to work it out *before* we get married. He doesn't need to be bothered with this."

Dr. Morris calmly yet firmly held his ground. "Our group therapy will be difficult. You'll need his support. You will *not* be able to make it on your own. You have to tell him."

I still hesitated, but he continued. "My next group won't begin for two months. That gives you plenty of time."

During the next couple of months I worked up my courage to take another painstaking step: Tell Bryce my ugly secret.

Sharing the Secret

"Bryce, I have something I need to tell you," I said with a quivering voice. "And I ... I just don't know how ..."

"Laura, ... you can tell me *anything,*" he said with those kind, puppy-dog eyes.

"I ... I mean, I have this ... problem," I hesitated. Tears rolled down my face, so I turned my head and covered my mouth.

"Honey, what is it?"

"I don't want to tell you this ugly thing about myself. You might stop loving me."

"Laura, *nothing* can ever come between us," he said as he gripped both my shoulders and looked me in the eyes. "I love you and *nothing* can ever change that."

Bryce was right.

After I revealed my nightmare to him, he held me in his arms and wept—then vowed to help me win this battle. It felt like a ton of boulders had been lifted from my head. And for the first time in my life, I had the hope to continue.

The Courage to Quit

I then began six months of intensive group therapy. Dr. Morris was right—it *was* difficult.

The first thing we had to do was remove our symptoms: taking laxatives, throwing up and any other means of getting rid of our food.

At every session we ate supper together. It was a nightmare. Sometimes it was a two-hour process. We sat around a large table and were required to eat everything on our plate. It was hard ... considering that this food couldn't be purged.

One particular evening the doctor placed a tray in front of each of us containing one cup of spaghetti, a half cup of green beans and a slice of garlic bread.

My eyes bugged out. *I can't eat all of this,* I thought. *I'll gain weight immediately!*

I had been used to consuming probably five times that much—but also getting rid of it. Since I was not allowed to do that anymore, I was terrified of eating an entire meal, even though it contained only 315 calories.

Six months of intensive therapy taught me how to see food in its proper perspective. I know now that for my 5'7" frame I can consume 1,800 to 2,400 calories per day, and if I exercise about three times a week, I won't gain because my body actually uses the nutrients I consume.

Facing the Future—With a Smile

When my group therapy concluded, I began six months of non-intensive therapy, going beneath the symptoms and learning *why* I did what I did. This helped me gain self-confidence and a greater ability to deal with the pressures and conflicts of life. One big struggle I tackled was my hard home life—and my messed-up dad.

I began to realize that my drive to be *perfect* centered on my *imperfect* dad. I desperately wanted to compensate for the disappointments at home, and sense my own self-worth. So I tried to fill the holes in my life by being the best at everything ... especially my appearance. That's when bulimia got its hold on me.

Thankfully, I got things in perspective and got out of the deadly cycle. The future finally looks bright—not perfect.

* * *

There is a newfound sense of freedom and hope in Laura's life—one which can only be perfected by a personal relationship with Jesus Christ. Laura's search for security was rooted in the desire for unconditional love and acceptance. In 1 John 4:7, the Bible states this love "comes from God."

And check this out: "This is how God showed his love among us: He sent his one and only Son into the world that we might live through him. This is love: not that we loved God, but that he loved us and sent his Son as an atoning sacrifice for our sins" (1 John 4:9-10).

* * *

Dangerous Abuses

"My friend only uses laxatives or throws up once in a while, like if she wants to lose five pounds for a date. That's not so bad, is it?"

Experimenting with laxatives, diuretics and vomiting—all of these things can be life-threatening. It's important that you understand the danger so you can share it with your friend.

The Danger of Vomiting
The acid in our stomach is strong enough to eat our skin and tear the enamel off our teeth. Excessive vomiting forces stomach acid into the esophagus, which causes pain and swelling in the throat. After a period of time one runs the risk of not only *tearing* the throat but rupturing the esophagus as well. Also, the more one vomits, the more scar tissue is built up in the esophagus, causing the throat to narrow. This makes it extremely difficult and painful to swallow.

The Danger of Laxatives
Laxative abuse, like excessive vomiting, can mess up the body's electrolytes. This means potassium is low. That's pretty critical because it's vital for our heart to function normally. Without the proper amount of potassium we lose respiratory function. Most anorexics die from heart failure—this is how it begins.

Karen Carpenter, a popular singer from the '70s, died from heart failure due to anorexia and laxative abuse. She had been released from the hospital and was *in recovery* when her heart stopped functioning due to the amount of damage that had already been done.

Continued excessive use of laxatives can also cause chronic constipation. There is no medication available that can treat this because of the total disruption of the body's normal electrical circuit. Our body needs to maintain the balance we were created with. When we cause our insides to become unbalanced, we're tampering with God's intricate and creative wiring system.

The Danger of Diuretics

Diuretics ("water pills") cause the kidneys to secrete larger than normal amounts of urine. This in turn causes an eloctrolyte imbalance and dehydration. Again, an electrolyte imbalance lowers your potassium, which causes heart failure.

"Wow! That's pretty serious! But what if I tell her about the dangers and she still doesn't stop?"

Whatever you do, don't ignore the problem or think it will go away by itself. It won't ... in fact, it may get worse as "once in a while" becomes more and more often. Here's what you can do!

1. Let your friend know you're aware of the problem.
2. Let her know there is hope.
3. Let her know there are treatment programs and counselors who can help.
4. Don't play "psychologist" ... you are not in a position to fix or save the person with an eating disorder.

Even though what your friend is doing is dangerous, it's important never to use a moral or judgmental tone in talking with your friend. When we make moral judgments we essentially say that someone is good or bad because of what she does or feels, or doesn't do or feel.

Here are some examples of moral judgments:

- "Why can't you just push away from the table?"
- "How can you do that to yourself?"
- "If you really cared about your family, you wouldn't do that."
- "You're certainly not living the way God wants you to live."

An eating disorder is not a moral problem; it is an addictive disorder.

"But my friend says she doesn't have an eating disorder 'cause she can stop any time she wants to."

There are all kinds of ways people with eating disorders rationalize what they are doing. By the time they admit they can't solve the problem themselves, it may be too late: Permanent damage may have already been done to their bodies.

Your friend battling anorexia or bulimia may have some twisted ideas such as:

1. "If I read the right book(s) I'll find the knowledge I need to recover from my eating disorder."
2. "I have to figure out a way to deal with this problem on my own; everyone else will think I'm a horrible person if they find out what I do or what I think."
3. "If I find the right diet (or nutritional information), I'll be

able to give up my eating disorder."

4. "If I can just get down to a certain weight, everything will be OK."

5. "I'll eventually outgrow this. I'm just going through a phase right now."

If you hear any of the above rationales from your friend, please lovingly, but firmly, tell her she is deceiving herself. Encourage her to seek professional help. Volunteer to go with her, if that will help.

"How can I tell if my friend has a real eating disorder, or if she's just being careful about controlling her weight?"

Here's a simple checklist to go through with your friend. Of course, this isn't the final word on eating disorders, but there's a possibility that if she checks several of the first eleven statements, she has an eating disorder. If she checks many of the statements, there's an excellent chance she has an eating disorder.

True or False.

___ I cannot control my eating.

___ I weigh several times a day.

___ If I could control my weight, everything else in my life would be great.

___ I'm overly controlled about my eating.

___ I avoid being around other people when I am feeling fat.

___ I have difficulty eating in front of other people, or I have trouble eating what I would like to eat when I am with others.

___ I exercise to make up for what I have eaten.

___ I usually eat for reasons other than hunger.

___ I take laxatives or diuretics to make up for what I have eaten.

___ I hide food.

___ If I can't eat perfectly, I might as well not follow a diet.

___ I will go to great lengths to avoid conflict.

___ I take care of everyone but me.

___ I am a "people pleaser."

___ I feel good knowing I am a perfectionist.

___ I often feel guilty or ashamed.

___ I deliberately stay very busy and am always in a hurry.

___ No one person really knows everything about me.

___ I find it hard to ask for help.

___ I am just existing.

___ I feel totally out of control.

___ Most people have no idea what I am feeling.

If your friend checked several of the above statements, she probably finds it extremely difficult to separate her self-esteem from her weight and from what the scale says. Let her know that you love her *no matter what she weighs!* Give her lots of hugs and bathe her in prayer!

"I'm still not sure if I know what to say or do to help my friend. Is there some place I can call for help?"

For information on programs for anorexia and bulimia, please contact Remuda Ranch, a Christian organization dedicated to helping teen girls and women overcome the battle.

Remuda Ranch
One East Apache
Wickenburg, AZ 85390
(Call 1-800-555-1212 for their toll-free number).

THREE

Help!
My Friend is Depressed!

Haley was an outgoing fifteen-year-old girl who was excited about heading to Latin America with several other teens under my care on a recent missions adventure. Prior to the trip, she had written me about her excitement of sharing Jesus with people in another country.

After a brief two-day training period in Miami, we boarded our all-night flight for our southbound destination. Only then did we learn that Haley was scared of flying. *Really* scared! She was beside herself—agitated, on edge and teary-eyed. I couldn't help but wonder why she hadn't told anyone about her fear *before* she decided to take the trip.

To the anxious and fearful Haley, nine hours seemed like an eternity. We finally arrived at our destination, made our way to our lodging and unpacked. I had barely put away my things when I noticed Haley sitting in a corner, weeping. Not sniffling like she had a cold—sobbing like her world had come to an end.

I sat on the floor next to her and asked her if she was home-sick. She could barely talk, but she managed to tell me she was.

"Well, it's OK to be homesick," I said. "I'm glad you have a family you're so close to that you miss them when you're apart. That's wonderful."

Knowing Haley hadn't really slept the night before, I encouraged her to turn in early and get as much sleep as she could before we headed out for ministry the next day. Haley went to bed, but she didn't get much sleep. Neither did her roommates. Haley kept them awake most of the night with her continuous weeping.

As the trip progressed, Haley's condition worsened. Most teens who are homesick call home, cry a bit and then get on with their purpose of being in a foreign country. Not Haley. She called home. A lot. But she wouldn't quit crying. I tried to get her to be specific about why she was crying, but without success. "Haley, we're only going to be here a week," I said. "You'll be with your family again before you know it."

She continued to sob.

"You can pick up the phone and call home as much as you want," I reminded her. "It's not like you're out of touch with your mom."

She continued to sob.

"Haley, why did you come on this missions trip?"

She continued to sob, but forced a few words through her tears: "I thought God wanted me to."

"Well, I believe he brought you here," I affirmed. "And he has you here for a specific purpose. Will you let him use you while you're here?"

She continued to sob.

"Haley, why are you crying? I mean, you knew when you came on this missions trip that you'd have to be away from your family for a week and a half, and that you'd be out of your comfort zone."

She continued to sob but pushed a few more words out of her mouth. "But I didn't know it was going to be *this* uncomfortable."

We were staying in a dorm-type building. I thought it was great. Everyone had beds, showers, toilets that worked, clean sheets and soap. I had stayed in some remote areas in primitive third-world villages that made this feel luxurious. I was having trouble identifying with Haley, but I wanted to help.

"Haley, we're in a great facility, we're safe, we've eaten good food. What's making you uncomfortable?"

"Well, I didn't know I was going to have to sleep on such a small bunk with such a hard, lumpy pillow!"

"Haley," I continued, "you're going to hold orphans in your lap tomorrow that don't even *have* a pillow. You'll see places that people are calling 'home' that we wouldn't even keep an animal in. I don't think your pillow is going to be that important after tomorrow."

But by the end of the next day, she was no better. Haley continued to sob incessantly. I really didn't understand, and since I didn't have much patience left, I asked our Christian medical doctor to see her. He told me that she was fine physically, but she definitely had some emotional problems. He told me she was depressed.

I then got her to a Christian counselor who talked with her for hours. The counselor told me the same thing: "Haley's depressed."

Why hadn't it surfaced earlier? I don't know. I can only suspect that the stress of being in a foreign country—and away from her loved ones—caused some things to surface that she hadn't experienced in the security of her tightly-knit family.

Haley spent the entire week and a half in tears. She was incapable of making any decisions at all. If I held up a Coke and a Pepsi and asked her which she wanted, she'd respond, "I don't know."

If I asked her if she wanted me to stick close to her the next day, she'd say, "I don't know."

When asked if she was ready for supper, you can guess what her response was, can't you? "I don't know."

It was as if she were turning into a vegetable. I was really confused . . . but Haley was depressed.

What Is Depression?

"What's it mean when someone is 'depressed'?"

Before we talk about what depression *is*, let's first agree on what it's *not*. Amber catches up with you in the hall after school. You ask how it's going, and she responds: "We just had a pop quiz in science. I could have pulled an A if I'd known about it, but I probably made a C. I'm so depressed!"

Is Amber really depressed? No. She's bothered, but she's not actually in a state of depression.

Morgan calls you later: "I just heard that Heath is taking Erin to the prom. You *know* how long I've had my eye on him. I am so-o-o-o depressed!"

Is Morgan truly depressed? No. She's bummed. She's sad. She may even be a little angry and jealous, but she's not actually in a state of depression.

We often use the term "depression" to describe a variety of feelings. Many times those feelings—sadness, grief, hopelessness, jealousy, anger, inferiority—can play a part in depression. Depression is nothing to laugh at. It affects millions of people around the world—good people, Christians, actors, musicians, accountants, teachers, pastors. Anyone can become depressed.

In order to help your friend through depression, it'll help first to understand a little about it. After all, there's more than one kind of depression.

A depressed mood: This is usually linked directly to a specific situation and isn't long-term. For instance, if you've recently experienced a breakup with your boyfriend, you may feel deep sadness and grief for a few weeks, but eventually you'll get back to being yourself again.

Clinical depression: When someone experiences this kind of depression, it's more persistent and severe, and it isn't always linked to a specific cause, as is a depressed mood. Clinical depression has a variety of symptoms and can include these specific types of depression: *major depressive disorder, dysthymic disorder* and *bipolar disorder.*

I know. I know. Suddenly this is sounding like a medical dictionary instead of specific ways you can help a hurting friend. But stick with me, OK? I'll make it easy to understand. I promise. (Remember: you're reading this because you care about someone you think is depressed. So keep going.)

Here are some common symptoms that someone will experience if she has a major depressive disorder. But don't get scared if you've felt some of these things, too! Someone with a major depressive disorder will experience at least five of these symptoms for more than two weeks in such a way that it interferes with her daily life. (That's a big difference!)

- Irritable or sad most days—all day long
- No longer interested in activities she once loved
- Weight loss (without trying to lose) or weight gain (more than 5 percent of body weight in one month); loss of appetite or increased appetite
- Not able to sleep, or sleeping too much nearly every day
- Feeling tired and worn out nearly all day, every day
- Restlessness

- Battling with huge amounts of guilt on a daily basis
- Feeling worthless—to the point of not being able to function with a positive demeanor
- Lack of ability to concentrate or make decisions
- Dwelling on thoughts of death or suicide

Dysthymic disorder: Teens with dysthymic disorder are usually cranky and hard to get along with as well as being depressed. They're usually negative, critical and have a hard time relating to people their own age as well as adults.

Teens battling a dysthymic disorder usually have depressive symptoms for at least a year. Some of these symptoms are the same as one who's experiencing a major depressive disorder:

- Low energy, tired a lot
- Can't sleep—or sleeps too much
- Not hungry—or always hungry
- Low self-esteem
- Difficulty making decisions; hard to concentrate
- Feeling hopeless

Bipolar disorder: During the teen years, it's common—and even expected—to have fluctuating moods. But if you have a friend who's struggling with a bipolar disorder, her mood swings go beyond the normal teen changes. Her changes in mood will go from being highly energetic (she'll talk constantly, have unending energy, not require much sleep, feel great about herself) to being majorly depressed to the point of not being able to function normally.

"What makes a person become depressed? Does it mean my friend is crazy?"

Depression is due to a variety of causes—not because your friend is bad or crazy. Sometimes the chemicals in our brain just get a little off-balance and we simply need to see a medical doctor who can prescribe medication to help realign those chemicals.

Sometimes depression is due to events that have happened in your friend's past, and she needs to see a counselor who can help pull out the buried hurt and show her how to deal with it. Other times, one will need medication *and* counseling to win the battle of depression.

"But I thought my friend was a Christian! How could she be depressed?"

It's a common mistake to think that Christians should never get depressed because we have Jesus. Isn't that a little like saying Christians should never get the flu because we have Jesus? If our physical bodies wear out and become ill, why is it so hard to realize that our emotions, our mind and our brain sometimes need extra help as well?

Of course, only a professional can truly diagnose depression, but here's a list of questions that may help you gain perspective on whether you or your friend may be experiencing depression. If you or your friend check yes to just one or two of these questions, you're experiencing sadness or anger. Everyone deals with that. But if you or your friend answers yes to *many*—and if you've experienced all of them close together (like in the past year), you are probably battling with depression.

Answer yes or no

____ Has there been a death in your family in the past year?

____ Has a close friend died during the past year?

____ Has your pet died or been lost in the past year?

____ Have you recently broken up with your boyfriend?

____ Do you have a close friend who has rejected or betrayed you in the past year?

____ Has one of your best friends moved away in the past year?

____ Have your folks separated or divorced in the past couple of years?

____ Have your folks been fighting a lot more than usual during the past year?

____ Do you see one of your parents a lot less than before?

____ Has your family gone through a financial crisis in the past year? (Has Mom or Dad lost a job, or has there been some other financial setback?)

____ Have you moved to a new location in the past year?

____ Have you changed schools in the past year?

____ Do you have a family member who has experienced serious depression in the past year?

____ Has a brother or sister left home (for college or a job, or to get married) in the past year?

____ Does anyone in your family abuse alcohol or drugs?

____ Do you have a family member who has been seriously injured in the past year?

____ Have you had an injury or an illness in the past year that has forced you to cut back on normal activities?

___ Do you have an ongoing illness (epilepsy, diabetes) that limits your activity with friends or is a source of arguments between you and your folks?

___ Have you had a lot of recent body changes (starting your period, breast development, tall growth spurt, etc.)?

___ Have you developed physically faster or slower than most of your friends, and do they tease you about it?

___ Do you usually maintain low self-esteem?

___ Are you extremely critical of yourself?

___ Do your folks place unreasonably high expectations on you and become upset when you don't meet those expectations?

___ Do you have a family member who is very critical of you?

___ Is it really tough to communicate right now with your folks? Are you yearning for a closeness that you used to enjoy with them?

___ Do you have a learning disability?

___ Is it hard for you to make or keep friends?

___ Do you find yourself wondering obsessively if your parents really care about you?

___ Are you feeling smothered by strict parents who don't allow you to express anger or share your opinions?

___ Are you being emotionally or physically abused by someone close to you?

___ Have you been sexually abused?

___ Do other students gang up on you and give you a hard time?

___ Do you feel like a failure when you do something that's less than your best—or when you make a grade that's not as high as you expected?

___ Have you had a run-in with one of your teachers this past year?

___ Has a stepparent been added to your family in the past year?

___ Has your immediate family increased during the past year due to a birth, adoption, grandparent moving in, etc.?

___ Do you have a brother or sister who has achieved so well in the past year that he or she has drawn your parents' attention excessively to them? Have your folks often made remarks such as, "If you were more like (your brother or sister) …"

___ Have you met a big goal recently (graduation, honors, special recognition) that has been exciting to you, but now that you've met it, you're feeling a letdown?

"Wow! My friend has had a lot of these things happen to her! OK, so how can I help?"

Be patient. Sometimes we love our friends so much, it's hard for us to be objective when it comes to helping them. You may *want* to try to "force" your friend to get help, but it really has to be her decision. Meanwhile, here are a few tips on what not to do and what can help.

Don't …

- Say, "Snap out of it!" Someone who's depressed *can't* snap out of it. She needs help.
- Say, "I just don't get you anymore. You're no fun."
- Ignore her.
- Give up on her.

```
┌─────────────────────────────────────────────────┐
│                      Do ...                       │
│  • Say, "I don't really understand, but I'm here  │
│    for you."                                      │
│  • Say, "Can we pray together regularly?"         │
│  • Give her space when she needs it.              │
│  • Give her lots of hugs.                         │
│  • Write her encouraging notes.                   │
│  • Encourage her to talk with a professional (a   │
│    pastor, a counselor, a doctor).                │
└─────────────────────────────────────────────────┘
```

So do not fear, for **I am with you;** do not be dismayed, for **I am your God.** I will strengthen you and help you; **I will uphold you** with my righteous right hand.

ISAIAH 41:10, emphasis mine

How can you help your friend through depression? Well, you're not a counselor, you're a *friend*. So don't pretend to know all the answers or try to diagnose the problem. Love her like Jesus loves her. Be there for her. And again, encourage her to seek professional help.

When a Friend Is Thinking of Suicide

Dear Susie:

I have a friend who's not very happy. She's threatened suicide before. I don't really think she'd go through with it, but I care about her and want to help. She just keeps saying that no one understands. Any ideas?

Meredith

Suicide threats are nothing to ignore or mess around with. Let your friend know that you're extremely concerned that she's making such disturbing statements.

I suggest you talk with an adult *immediately.* Seek advice from your parents, your pastor or your school counselor, but DO tell an adult! This is too big for you to handle without adult intervention.

Probably the worst feeling in the world is not being understood by those around us, so I really feel for your friend. Please remind her, though, that Jesus reallyreallyreally *does* understand! He knows exactly how she feels and what she's going through.

Your friend needs you to be "Jesus with skin on." Can you do that? Will you ask God to help you love her as he himself loves her? Don't be afraid to put your arm around her shoulders. Hug her. Send her encouraging notes.

There's probably a *reason* she's feeling no one understands. You might ask her: "Is it because you haven't *tried* communicating with anyone?" (When we're depressed, it's often tempting to stuff our feelings deep inside.)

"Maybe you *have* tried communicating your hurt, but haven't communicated it effectively. Are you trying to share your thoughts and feelings when you're angry? Are you really saying what you mean? Are you beating around the bush, making people try to guess what's bothering you?"

Encourage her to keep *trying* to communicate with those around her until she finds someone who will listen and understand. Remind her that you're more than willing to be that person for her. But also know that she needs counseling. After all, you don't know what she's struggling with, and if she's threatening suicide, that's too big for you to handle on your own!

FOUR

Help!
My Friend's Addicted to the Internet

With the information superhighway, we now have access to places we've never been and we have options we've never had before. With a few simple clicks I can virtually be anywhere in the world.

I recently went to the most primitive place in the world—Irian Jaya. Cannibals still live on this island and researchers remain in the process of counting and recording tribes. I had to take twenty flights in twelve days to get there and back. Once in Irian Jaya, I took a small plane and flew over rain forests and tropical jungles to a tiny village called Wahuka inhabited by the Kirikiri tribe.

These folks have never heard of electricity, refrigerators, bathtubs or bicycles. They're still living in the Stone Age, using pieces of rock attached by twine to sticks to accomplish their tasks.

Now, I'm not a big computer whiz. I'm really not. I know how to send e-mail, and I can surf the Web (with a little help). But I'm in constant amazement that I can sit at my desk in Colorado Springs, turn on my computer and with a few clicks and entries find out what the exact temperature is on any given day in villages similar to Wahuka! It's incredible! It's fantastic!

But it's also frightening. With *so* much to access at our fingertips, we often overlook the danger of becoming *too involved* with the Internet. It's easy to become "hooked" on chat rooms and communicating with people who can't see you.

You may have a friend who has fallen into this trap. Please take it seriously. The Internet can be dangerous. And becoming obsessed with communicating with someone on-line can actually hamper relationships with the friends you *can* see.

Check out this letter I received from a gal who's worried about her friend.

Dear Susie:

I have a friend who loves to visit chat rooms on her computer. She'll rush home from volleyball and go straight to her computer. Even when we're in youth group, she's constantly thinking about logging on when she gets home. I'm worried about her. Can't that be dangerous?

Frightened in Calgary, Alberta

I'm glad you're concerned about her. Yes, it can be dangerous—extremely dangerous—to be that involved in chat rooms. God wants us to live well-balanced lives and not be obsessive about anything.

Many teens, without even realizing it, have given out too much information on-line to strangers who later began stalking them (or even worse).

When you're on-line, there's a false sense of security of being able to "talk" with someone who can't see you and who doesn't really know you. It feels safe to tell this person anything—what you're feeling, what you're struggling with and what your dreams for the future are.

The danger, though, comes in the fact that you have no clue who the other person is. He may *tell* you he's your age, that he goes to church and lives far away. But he may actually be twice your age, living in your same town and involved in pornography or other dangerous activities.

Please show the following story to your friend and try to convince her to not be so obsessive about getting on-line.

This Could Happen To You
by Helen Walden and Sharon Sipos

*If you ever go on-line, use e-mail or
yak it up in chat rooms, you've got to read this!*

Shannon could hear the footsteps behind her as she walked home. The thought of being followed made her heart beat faster. "You're being silly," she told herself. "No one's following you."

Just to be safe, she began to walk faster, but the footsteps kept up with her pace. Shannon said a quick prayer, "God, please keep me safe." She saw the porch light burning and ran the rest of the way to her house.

Once inside, she leaned against the door for a moment, relieved to be in the safety of her home. She glanced out the window to see if anyone was there. The sidewalk was empty.

After tossing her books on the sofa, Shannon decided to grab a snack and get on-line. There she could talk to strangers without being afraid. After all, no one knew who she really was, and no one could hurt her.

She logged on under her screen name, ByAngel213. Checking her Buddy List she saw GoTo123 was on. She sent him an instant message.

ByAngel213: Hi. I'm glad you're on! I thought someone was following me home today. It was really weird!

GoTo123:   LOL. You watch too much TV. Why would someone be following you? Don't you live in a safe neighborhood?

Shannon smiled at the computer code, LOL: *laugh out loud.*

ByAngel213:   I guess it was my imagination ... 'cause I didn't see anybody when I looked out.

GoTo123:   Unless you gave your name on-line.... You haven't done that have you?

ByAngel213:   Of course not. I'm not stupid, you know.

GoTo123:   Did you have a softball game after school today?

ByAngel213:   Yes, and we won!

GoTo123:   What's your team called?

ByAngel213:   We're the Canton Cats. We have tiger paws on our uniforms. They are really kewl.

GoTo123:   Do you pitch or what?

ByAngel213:   No. I play second base. I've got to go. My homework has to be done before my parents get home. I don't want them mad at me ... Bye

GoTo123:   Catch you later ... Bye

Friend or Foe?

GoTo123 decided it was time to teach ByAngel213 a lesson—one she'd never forget. He went to the member menu and began to search for her profile. When it came up, he highlighted it and printed it out. He took out a pen and began to write down what he knew about Angel213 so far.

Name:	Shannon
Birthday:	Jan 3, 1985
Age:	14
State where she lives:	North Carolina
Hobbies:	softball, chorus, skating and going to the mall

Along with this information, he knew she lived in Canton. She'd just told him that. He knew she stayed by herself until 6:30 every evening until her parents came home from work. He knew that she played softball on Thursday afternoons on the school team, the Canton Cats. Her favorite number, seven, was printed on her jersey. He knew she was in the eighth grade at Canton Middle School.

Shannon gave all of this information to GoTo123 in the conversations they'd had on-line. He had enough information to find her now. *She'll be so surprised,* he thought. *She doesn't even know what she's done.*

The Search Is On

Shannon didn't tell her parents about the incident on the way home from the ballpark that day. She didn't want them to get hysterical and stop her from walking home from the softball games. Parents were always overreacting and hers were the worst. It made her wish she was not an only child. Maybe if she'd have had brothers and sisters her parents wouldn't be so overprotective.

By Thursday, Shannon had forgotten about the footsteps following her. Her game was in full swing when suddenly she felt someone staring at her. It was then that the memory came back.

She glanced up from her second-base position to see a man watching her closely. He was leaning against the fence behind first base, and he smiled when she looked at him. He didn't look scary, so she quickly dismissed the fear she'd felt.

After the game, he sat on the bleachers while she talked to her coach. She noticed his smile once again as she walked past him. He nodded and she smiled back. He noticed her number on the back of the shirt. He knew he'd found her. Quietly, he walked a safe distance behind her. He didn't want to frighten her or have to explain to anyone what he was doing.

It was only a few blocks to Shannon's home. Once he saw where she lived, he quickly returned to the park to get his car. Now he had to wait. He decided to get a bite to eat until the time came to go to Shannon's house. He drove to a fast-food restaurant and sat there until it was time to make his move.

A Life-Saving Lesson

Shannon was in her room later that evening when she heard voices in the living room. "Shannon, come here," her father called. He sounded upset and she couldn't imagine why. She went into the room to see the man from the ballpark sitting on the sofa.

"Sit down," her father began. "This man is a retired police-man, and he's just told us a most interesting story about you."

Shannon moved cautiously to a chair across from the man. *How could he tell my parents anything?* she thought. *I've never seen him before today!*

"Do you know who I am, Shannon?" the man asked.

"No," she answered.

"I'm your on-line friend, GoTo123."

Shannon was stunned. "That's impossible! GoTo123 is a kid about my age! He's fifteen and lives in Michigan!"

The man smiled. "I know I told you that, but it wasn't true.

You see, Shannon, there are people on-line who pretend to be kids; I was one of them.

"But while others do it to find kids and hurt them, I belong to a group of parents who do it to protect kids from predators. I came here tonight to let you know how dangerous it is to give out too much information to people on-line.

"You told me enough about yourself to make it easy for me to find you: your name, the school you go to, the name of your ball team and the position you play. The number on your jersey just made finding you a breeze."

Shannon was stunned. "You mean you don't live in Michigan?"

He laughed. "No, I live in Raleigh. It made you feel safe to think I was so far away, didn't it?"

She nodded.

"I had a friend whose daughter was like you. Only she wasn't as lucky. The guy found her and murdered her while she was home alone. Kids are taught not to tell anyone when they are alone, yet they do it all the time on-line.

"The wrong people trick you into giving out information on-line—a little here and a little there. Before you know it, you've told them enough for them to find you without even realizing you've done it. I hope you've learned a lesson from this and won't do it again."

"I won't," Shannon promised.

"And will you tell others about this so they'll be safe, too?"

"It's a promise!"

That night Shannon told her parents about thinking someone had followed her home the week before. They listened as she assured them it had been her imagination, and she promised to tell them if anything like that happened again. Tears formed in her eyes as she recalled the prayer she'd prayed.

"You know," she said solemnly, "I asked God to keep me safe and he really has, hasn't he?"

How to Avoid Having This Happen to You

So, how much are you telling your on-line friends? Could someone find you if he or she wanted to? How much do you really know about the people you're talking with?

The story you just read isn't true. Yet it could have happened; it was based on true information given out to us by people on-line. It could easily happen to anyone who chats freely with strangers.

While it's not meant to frighten you, it *is* a lesson on how to be safe when you're on-line. This message is for guys as well as girls. Guys have been victims of on-line predators, too. So grab all your friends—guys and girls—and share the following guidelines for protecting yourself.

1. If you ever get aggressive, angry or abusive messages, tell your parents at once. Contact your Internet provider for assistance.

2. You probably won't like this, but we strongly suggest that you avoid chat rooms altogether. Experts agree that chat rooms are by far the most dangerous Internet activity, for the reasons that were shown through our story.

3. Never tell anyone your full name, address, phone number, city or any other personal information about yourself or your family.

4. If you use America Online or CompuServe, watch what information you include on your profile. Don't put your date of birth, especially the year. If you use Netscape, Explorer or Mosaic to connect through a local service provider, don't enter your full name—especially your last

name—when you configure the software for e-mail and news groups. This also applies if you use a separate program to get your e-mail. Many people know how to get your street address armed with nothing but your last name and the name of your service provider. Remember, you don't have to give out any information you don't want to.

5. If you still choose to be in a chat room or are using e-mail and someone asks you personal questions, such as where you go to school, where you live or any other personal questions you don't feel comfortable answering, don't hesitate to write, "I'm sorry, I don't give out personal information" or "My parents have asked me not to tell that."

6. If someone sends you an e-mail form with personal information about himself or herself on it and suggests you fill one out just like it, be alerted and don't do it. You have no idea to whom or where it will be forwarded!

7. If, once again, you decide to be in a chat room and anyone pressures you to talk, won't leave you alone or asks for personal information, get off-line immediately.

8. Don't respond to e-mail from people you don't know. If you believe you've received something strange, tell your parents.

9. Never agree to meet anyone whom you've met on-line face-to-face.

"But what if I've already given out some of this information? What should I do?"

For your own safety, tell your parents. You may also write us with any questions or suggestions at:

TeenFocus@aol.com or
TeenFocus1@aol.com

Who Are We?
We are two mature, dedicated Christians who have a real concern for the safety of young people on-line. We've recently witnessed several instances where young people have given out or been asked to give out all kinds of personal information. The people asking for this information were strangers. Because of this, we've formed a group called Teen Focus. We hope to send out a newsletter on a regular basis with fun and safe things teens can participate in on the Web.

In the world of the Internet, people can say they are anyone they want—and none of us have any way of knowing who they really are. We want to help you. Please show this article to your parents and pass it along to any friends you think may benefit from it.

* * *

For more information on this subject, check out Focus on the Family's CitizenLink Internet resource page on the Web at:
www.family.org/cforum/research/papers/a000z689.html

---

*"I don't do chat rooms, but I have
a friend who does. She laughs
when I tell her it's dangerous.
How can I convince her?"*

I'm glad you're concerned about your friend. You have reason to be. I'm also proud of you for wanting to help her. First, show her the above story, then get together and talk about it. Ask her how she felt after she read the story. Point out that serious crimes are being committed daily by folks taking advantage of teenagers through the Internet.

Next, ask her if you can hold her accountable to do the following:

- Begin to limit her involvement on the Internet gradually. For example, suggest that she not even turn her computer on for two days this week. Hold her accountable. On those two days, get together and pray with her. Next week she gives up chat rooms, etc.

  Again, pray together as she releases this involvement to God. She's giving something up that she's enjoying, so she may be angry, sad, frustrated. And she may take some of those emotions out on you. That's OK. Be prepared. Continue to pray with her.

- Help your friend find other activities to replace her time spent on the Internet. Start a Bible study together. Learn a new hobby. Look for a part-time job together. Take a pottery class.

- Continue to stick close to your friend, even after she's given up her involvement on the Internet. Keep holding her accountable in a gentle way. Ask her to let you know when she's tempted to fall back into a chat room. That temptation will probably hit her when she's feeling lonely or sad. Be there for her.

Computers are incredible machines. Make it your goal to help your friend find *balance*. In other words, don't expect her to never turn on her computer again. There are so many advantages to having the information superhighway and the access we have. She'll need that information for school and research. The key, though, is balance. Encourage her to continue using the computer to enhance her knowledge and improve her schoolwork, but to steer away from chat rooms and on-line relationships.

FIVE

Help!
My Friend Is Coping With an Illness!

Brooke and Keisha had been friends for three years when Keisha was diagnosed with diabetes. "She started pulling away from me," Brooke says. "Keisha became kind of angry and distant. I want her to know that we're still best friends. OK, so she's got diabetes. Our friendship shouldn't have to suffer. I care about Keisha, and I want to help her through this time of adjustment."

Maybe you, like Brooke, have a friend who's trying to cope with an illness or disease. The key word that Brooke used is "adjustment." As your friend learns how to adjust her lifestyle to necessary changes, you may need to give a little more in order to help her adjustment go more smoothly.

For example, Keisha now has to eat a balanced diet on a very regular schedule. She also has to test her blood sugar level and give herself insulin injections. She'll need some space at first. Allow her time to get used to this. She's going through some major changes.

Some adjustments are harder to make than others. A friend who has epilepsy may not be able to get her driver's license. Realize, as you reach out to your friend, that she's dealing with some major disappointment. How would *you* feel if you'd had your heart set on driving and recently found out you'd have to give up that dream?

It's also tough on your friend with special needs to realize she doesn't always fit in. Maybe she can't swim because she's confined to a wheelchair. Or perhaps she can't participate in team sports due to her blindness. Whatever the illness or disease, your friend probably feels isolated a lot and goes through more hurt than she's letting on.

You can be an encouragement to her. *You* can help her realize that God can use every illness, each setback, every handicap to bring glory to him.

I met seventeen-year-old Nann when she stopped by my office at *Brio* magazine. As she began telling our staff about herself, we decided to turn on the tape recorder so we could share her story with others. Check it out.

Here I Am!

Saying "It's what's on the inside that counts"
is one thing. Believing *it and living it are another.*
by Marty McCormack

"Ugh! I'm having such a *bad* hair day!"

Remember mumbling these words under your breath as you headed to school last week, and the countless times you repeated them as you stood in front of the bathroom mirror with your friends, desperately doing whatever you could to remedy the horrible situation surrounding your head?

Most of us have had days when we've been less than thrilled with our uncooperative hair. *Some* of us have gone so far as to consider chopping it all off. But not *all* of us.

Eighteen-year-old Nann Chafin is one girl who's not complaining about her hair. That's because since she was twelve, Nann hasn't had much hair to complain about. Within a few months of her hairstylist first discovering a dime-sized bald spot on the back of her head, Nann went from a full head of thick, blond curls to a head with a few strands of hair here and there.

Upon noticing the initial bald spot in August 1993, Nann's hairstylist said it looked like *alopecia areata,* an autoimmune deficiency, and suggested she visit a dermatologist. Nann's mom called a doctor from the salon, and after a consultation the dermatologist confirmed that Nann had *alopecia areata.*

The Scoop on Alopecia

So what does it mean to have an auto-immune deficiency that makes your hair fall out? Simply, it means that Nann's immune system thinks she's allergic to her own hair. There are different varieties of *alopecia.* Nann has *totalis*—it affects only her head. People who have *universalis alopecia* lose all their hair— eyebrows, eyelashes, leg hair, etc. Others who have less severe cases resulting in a patch of missing head hair or arm hair may not even realize they have *alopecia.*

Because *alopecia* is so rare, and because it is not life-threatening, the government hasn't allocated much money to research the condition. No one knows how or why a person may have it, and without much research, no great strides have been made in finding a helpful treatment or cure.

Though Nann says she wasn't worried about the first bald spot even when it grew to the size of a silver dollar, her dermatologist must have been. She immediately gave Nann more than thirty different medications to take at the same time.

"I became really weak from all the steroids, and I blew up like a balloon," Nann says. Even though she's no longer taking all the medication, Nann still has a lot of pain in her joints, a side effect of this condition. She expects she'll have some type of arthritis for the rest of her life.

More Than a Bad Hair Day

By January 1994, Nann's head was covered with bald spots. As her hair began to thin, she accumulated a collection of hats and got permission to wear them to her public school.

"For a long time I had a little bit of hair on the side of my head," Nann explains. "I could tease that and curl it and make it look like I had a little bit more hair than I did.

"I wore hats, but kids can be cruel. I remember this guy came up and jerked my hat off. People were standing around, and then all of a sudden they just stopped and stared. It was like they didn't know if they should do something, or if they should laugh. Some *did* laugh.

"I said to this guy, 'Are you finished?' He snickered and tried to be cool. So I said, 'Can I have my hat back, please?' He reluctantly returned it, and I put it back on. I said goodbye and walked down the stairs.

"It was the end of the school day, and I went home and told my mom, 'I'm not going back.' She woke me up the next morning for school, and I said, 'Mom, I'm not going back.' She said, 'OK, we'll get the necessary papers to school you at home.'"

In Search of One True Friend

Before Nann opted for homeschooling, she was involved with several activities at her school. Even while she was dealing with the effects of *alopecia* and the medications she was taking, she didn't let her pain keep her from making worthwhile contributions.

When Nann realized there wasn't a student choir at her school, she recruited an interested teacher and some students, and went before the school board and principal to request a choir. Today the school has a chorus program and Nann is invited to come back for concerts.

Nann says students thought a lot of her—when she had a full head of hair. Instead of having just *one* group of friends, she was in *every* group. During lunch she'd often move from table to table to visit with as many people as possible.

But once she started losing her hair, Nann began losing "friends" too. "I used to have a seat saved for me all the time at lunch," she remembers. "Once I started losing my hair and wearing hats to school, I'd walk up and there'd be no seats.

"When I'd sit down, people would literally get up and move. Even when we'd be walking somewhere, everyone would get in this huddle with their backs to me and leave me completely out.

"I basically had the same people in all my classes, and they didn't talk to me anymore. Whenever I'd put my fingers through my hair or put it behind my shoulder to lean down, I'd have to shake hair off. People complained about getting hair on their desk. When something like this happens, you really find out who your true friends are."

As if classes and lunchtime being unbearable weren't enough, Nann had to deal with insensitivity from teens during other parts of the school day as well. "Girls would go into the bathroom after lunch to brush their hair and freshen up for the rest of the day. When *I* did that, it was just embarrassing," she says.

"I wouldn't try to brush my hair, but I'd wait for other girls to do theirs. They'd say, 'Oh, I *hate* my hair! It never does anything right." I'd stand there thinking, *If you only knew....*"

Looking for the Bright Side

When Nann finally decided she'd had enough of public school, her dermatologist reluctantly signed her homebound papers. She hesitated because she thought Nann needed to get on with her life and be out in public. To Nann's dermatologist, dealing with *alopecia* seemed like no big deal. She didn't understand the middle-school world Nann lived in, which put so much importance on a person's outer appearance.

Once Nann was away from daily contact with other teens, she realized just how much she depended on God. "I know God helped me through everything," she says.

"It's been hard to explain because it's so personal—between God and me. I finally figured out that he helped me one day at a time. Sometimes for an hour at a time. He helped me little by little.

"I never, *never* let go of God. I never doubted him. But sometimes I'd get frustrated. Sometimes I'd think, *I know what I don't have.... I don't have my hair, I don't have my friends at school, I don't even have school anymore.*

"One day, I decided to sit down and think of what I *did* have. I thought and I thought. Finally I just said, 'I've got God. That's what I've got. I've got God, and my youth group, and my family.'

"What in the world would I do if I let go of God? What would I have? I'd have just this negative, nothing. I'd probably be in a fetal position on the floor somewhere, all depressed. Thank God that he didn't let *me* let go of *him*."

While Nann is highly involved in her youth group, she says she still goes for days without getting one phone call from a friend. Sometimes she thinks friends in her church don't realize that they're even more valuable to her now since she doesn't have connections with teens at school anymore.

"I'd love to have friends call and tell me what happened at school, or have them ask about my day at homeschool," she says. "Sometimes the support just isn't there. It still comes down to one or two. God, and one or two people."

Firm Foundation

Once during a service at church, Nann went to the altar for prayer. "I told my pastor, 'I want you to pray for my *alopecia*.' He started praying for me, but the entire prayer was for my 'Aunt Patricia.' I was laughing, and he thought I was crying and was patting my back."

Along with prayer, whether for her *alopecia* or nonexistent Aunt Patricia, Nann has gained much of her strength through Scripture. Paraphrasing Psalm 46, Nann says, "I love how it says, 'Nations will rise up against you and mountains will crumble,' and all of a sudden he says, 'Be still, and know that I am God.' When it gets to that part, peace comes over me. 'Just be still, and know that I am God, and I am here.' That's all I need to know.

"I just read somewhere that faith is neither sight, nor sense, nor reason, but just simply believing in God. Just believe in God. Faith the size of a mustard seed can move mountains, so if just believing in God can move mountains, think what can happen if you believe that God can perform miracles!"

She's Back!

Before Nann left South Carolina to visit the *Brio* staff in Colorado, she said something to her youth pastor that blew

him away. "When I come back," she said, "I might stop wearing my wig."

When Nann showed up in *Brio* land, she was without the
wig, but wore a purple scarf wrapped around her head. It
matched her sweater perfectly. A few weeks after we met Nann,
her mom wrote to fill us in on how Nann was doing. Here's an
excerpt from her letter.

> I must give you this update on Nann. Her interview has
> inspired and strengthened her. When we returned home, she
> found the courage to go before her youth group and share a
> little of what she's been through. She then told of her desire
> to not wear her wig anymore around them. Many of them
> didn't even know she wore a wig.
>
> With tears streaming down her face, Nann said, "I'm not
> wearing my wig anymore, and I need to know it's all right
> with all of you." Sobbing, she reached up and slowly, delib-
> erately, took off her hair in front of more than fifty teens and
> adults.
>
> That night, with the strength from God through the
> encouragement of her interview with *Brio,* Nann was free
> from bondage—after five years we feel our Nann is back.
> She's bruised and broken, but brave, strong and once again
> flashing that huge smile with freedom behind it.
>
> Sometimes God chooses not to physically heal, but he
> always heals in his own way and chooses our paths for his
> glory!

* * *

If you'd like more information about *alopecia areata,* write
to the National Alopecia Areata Foundation at P.O. Box
150760, San Rafael, CA 94915-0760.

Life Lessons From Nann

Since we met Nann two years ago, a lot of exciting things have happened in her life! She has received numerous invitations for speaking engagements and enjoys sharing her testimony wherever God opens a door.

Nann is going without her wig every day now. Well, almost every day—she *does* put it on occasionally for fun. Nann completed her senior year of high school at a local Christian school and graduated with sixty in her class. She is currently attending college and enjoying making new friends.

Even though she has had many exciting opportunities in the past couple of years, she's experienced some difficult times, too. A few months ago, she spent time in the hospital battling mono-hepatitis with pneumonia.

With all that Nann has experienced in going from a sought-after beauty pageant contestant to a teen without hair, you'd expect that she's learned something about life. Well, she has. Here are some thoughts she has to share with you.

On accepting people as they are: "I've learned that people can accept somebody in a wheelchair, or somebody without an arm, but when I come in without hair, it's like 'Oh, she looks so-o-o sick. What's wrong with her? Better not get too close....'

"When you meet someone who's going through a battle, just accept it and be a friend. I'd much rather have people come up to me and say, 'How'd you lose your hair?' than just stare or give me funny looks."

About true beauty: "The things of this world absolutely do not matter. I've been in beauty pageants. In fact, the Miss America

Pageant contacted me many times asking me to represent South Carolina. I never responded.

"We put so much focus on appearances. I've won first place in talent competitions and have been so active in school, but when it comes right down to where the rubber hits the road, all that matters is faith in God."

On facing challenges: "For those who have any kind of a challenge—physical or emotional—try not to get mad at God and ask, 'Why me? Why did this happen to me?' You need to know God is not trying to punish you because you're not good enough. He thinks you *are* good enough. You are good enough for him to be able to place a challenge before you, knowing that you can handle it and take it like a woman!

"Have your week of grieving over it, because you need that grieving and closure. Then go out there and say, 'OK, I'm finished with all the crying. God, what do you want me to do with this? Show me how you want me to use this.' The hard times are going to come, and they're going to be awful, but God can help you through it if you have that kind of an attitude.

"God has placed every situation and every detail of everything that you go through there for a reason. One day he'll place something in your life, and you'll think, *This is why God has given me this.* And it will be worth every bit of the struggle.

"For me, that time is when I give my testimony and people come up to me and say, 'God sent you here just for me.' The first time I gave my testimony, a lady leaned over behind me and said in my ear, 'I've been contemplating suicide, and you changed my mind completely.'

"Of course, that was God through me, but when she said

that, I was thinking, *It's worth everything, then, I've saved a life! God saved a life through me.*"

"My **grace** is sufficient for you, for my **power** is made **perfect** in **weakness**." —Jesus Christ
2 CORINTHIANS 12:9, emphasis mine

"Susie, my friend Amanda just found out she has leukemia. Like Nann, she's going to lose all her hair ... and maybe even her life! She's so depressed, she says she's mad at God for letting this happen to her. I just don't know what to do or say to help her. Help!"

Not everyone is able to rise above her illness as Nann did, maintaining such a positive attitude while struggling with a disease, especially a life-threatening disease.

Your friend sounds as though she is struggling to come to terms with her illness. Remember, God is big enough and loving enough to handle Amanda's doubts. This is not the time to get into a theological debate with your friend. Right now God has brought you into her life to be Jesus to her. He wants you to encourage her and to be patient as she juggles doubts and confusion. How? Here are a few things that might help.

Don't:

- Say, "Children are starving overseas, and you're worried about *your* illness?"
- Say, "It must be God's will."
- Ignore her pain or illness. Acting like it doesn't exist won't make it go away or help her feel any better.
- Bring special attention to her pain or illness.
- Get mad at her if she questions why God allows her illness.
- Abandon her if she doesn't get better after you pray for her.

Do:

- Take your cues from her. If she is weak and needs to rest a while before you continue shopping at the mall, sit with her.
- Understand that she has limitations. Accept them.
- Genuinely affirm her. Does her hair look especially nice today? Tell her. She aced the English test? Brag on her. She's especially good with children? Point that out to her.
- Laugh a lot together.

An anxious heart weighs a man down, but **a kind word cheers** him up.

PROVERBS 12:25, emphasis mine

Dear Susie:

My friend has cancer, and I feel at a loss for words. I want to minister to her and keep being her friend, but I'm not sure how.

Katrina

If I were battling cancer, you're exactly the kind of friend I'd want by my bedside! I admire your tenderness.

There are times when words simply can't express what we're feeling. It sounds like this is the case between you and your friend. Probably the very best way you can minister to her is simply to be near her. If she's not in too much pain, you may want to hug her gently or hold her hand.

If she wants to talk, be willing to listen. Ask if she has a favorite book she'd like you to read aloud for her. Or maybe she has some Scripture underlined in her Bible that you could read to her. Be willing to do anything necessary, but also learn to be comfortable doing nothing but simply being together. God bless you!

> The purposes of a man's heart are deep waters, but a man of **understanding** draws them out.
>
> PROVERBS 20:5, emphasis mine

"Susie, I found out today that my friend is never going to get better. She's dying, and I don't know what to do or say. Can you help me?"

Facing a terminal illness takes a great deal of courage, and your friend needs your support. Here are some things that might help.

- Read Scripture to her as she rests in bed.
- Rent her favorite video, and watch it together.
- Ask her to help you list her favorite memories of friends and family members. You do the writing and let her do all the talking.
- Pray for her—aloud—by her bedside.
- What else? Your turn. C'mon! Think of a few more things you can do for her, and get busy enjoying them.

As we close this chapter, I'd like to introduce you to another young lady whose strong relationship with Christ gives her the strength needed to juggle a terminal illness.

Blessing in Disguise
by Becky Clemmons

In 1982, at the age of five months, doctors told my parents I wouldn't live to see my first birthday. I was diagnosed with the fatal disease cystic fibrosis (CF). I did live to celebrate my first birthday, however, as well as my second and third and fourth—actually I've seen sixteen birthdays come and go.

I was hospitalized seventeen times before I turned fourteen, and I've been in thirteen more times since then. Most of these hospitalizations have been three to four weeks at a time. That means for a good part of my life, I've spent about every other month in the hospital. I do chest physiotherapy and nebulized breathing treatments twice daily, take thirty pills a day and get additional medicines intravenously every weekend. Every weekday I receive therapy at BroMenn Hospital in my home-town, on weekends I do more at home.

I make the four-hour trip to the doctor in Iowa City often and still have to keep up my schoolwork in order to graduate in two more years. I missed about three-fourths of my freshman year due to hospitalizations. I had to continue to do schoolwork into the summer so I wouldn't have to repeat that year.

I've had to grow up very quickly in my sixteen years and have had to face the fact that the average life expectancy for a child with CF is only thirty years. I know that CF is the number-one genetic killer of children and young adults in the United States. I've had to watch many of my teenage friends with CF die—some who have appeared to be healthier than I am. I've had to understand that next time it could be me.

Life With God

I'd like to tell you that this was my life *before* God ... but I can't. This is my life *with* God. You hear stories of tragedies and then hear at the end of the stories that the people found God and their lives completely turned around with no more worries or troubles—and this is wonderful. It's healing to hear people's stories and think that others just need to find God and everything *will* be wonderful. Unfortunately, I am not one of those people.

I grew up in a Christian home knowing that an early death could be my fate. I could have chosen to let myself go and feel sorry for myself. But someone told me that God had something more than just a life with an illness planned for me. I believe with all my heart that I was given this disease for a purpose. I believe I was given this so I could tell all of you that even with a disease like the one I have, I still have a wonderful life with God and I am still an optimist. I have seen a lot of non-Christian psychiatrists who can't believe that a person my age with this disease can be so positive. They think that I'm only denying the inevitable.

But they don't know why I can be this positive. They don't *know* the Great Physician. They don't understand why I'm not afraid of death, even though I know I could die at any time, because they don't know the loving and powerful God I do. They don't realize that the reason I'm always smiling is because the joy of the Lord truly is my strength.

The Best Is Yet to Come

Doctors haven't found a cure for CF yet, and my insurance company hasn't been too glad to pay my bills, but I still have hope. I hope that doctors will find a cure, but I also know that no matter what, a time will come when I won't have to deal with any of this anymore.

Heaven is a wonderful place where there are no more troubles, no more worries, no more heartaches and no more diseases. I look forward to the day when I can see the Great Physician's face and thank him for giving me this.

I have helped people to know that there really is a God who loves *everybody*. He didn't give me this disease because he wanted to hurt me. Instead, I believe he allowed me to have this *gift* so I could touch others' lives—like yours—and let *you* know that no matter what, Someone is always there for you. And Someone is always there to listen when you have problems, joys and tears.

"My friend Erica, who's in a wheelchair from a car crash, thinks her life is over and she'll never be able to help anyone else ever again. How can I help my friend to see that she can still help others?"

Try to help Erica realize that God can use her to help others who are struggling. Encourage her to talk openly about how she feels physically and emotionally. If she agrees, help her jot down some of the things she's learning through her experience.

She may not be ready to share her story right away. She still has to adjust to her new situation, and this takes time. But the time may come when she feels ready to share her testimony with other people. Ask her to practice giving her testimony in front of you. If she's open to it, suggest to your youth pastor that she share with your youth group. In the meantime, look for other fun things and service opportunities that you can do together!

Seventeen-year-old Amy Graham, who was born with no thumbs, is living proof that every person is capable of helping someone else. It wasn't always easy. In first grade, kids would say things like, "Eeew, don't touch me. You don't have thumbs." Or, "Give me five—oh wait, you can't." Amy learned early on what being made fun of was all about. But she kept a positive attitude. Sometimes when kids first noticed that she didn't have thumbs she'd respond with, "Oh, I left them at home in my drawer," or she'd act incredibly surprised and say, "Oh, my! I don't have thumbs!"

When Amy reached junior high, it became harder to deal with painful comments. "My seventh-grade science teacher pointed me out during class one time when he was talking about deformities. He said, 'Yeah, like Amy. Amy's deformed and abnormal.'"

When she entered high school, she decided to deepen her relationship with Christ. "I was a Christian in junior high, but since I wasn't spending time with God like I should have been, I always felt like I was missing something," she says. "I finally realized that nothing could fill my life—drugs, alcohol, friends, being popular, looking good—except God."

Amy has also battled feelings of inferiority toward her sister. "She's absolutely gorgeous!" she says. "I always felt inferior to her because she's older and really beautiful, *and she has thumbs!* It took me awhile to realize that God has made me a special person, too.

"God continues to teach me that our inner beauty is *so* much more important than our outer beauty. Everything on our outside can fade away; we grow older, we get wrinkly, we're not always young and youthful-looking.

"But inside we either grow stronger or we fall away. Staying close to God is so much more important than chasing outer beauty because that relationship is what's going to stay with you always."

As Amy has accepted herself for who God created her to be, she has come to count her uniqueness as a blessing. "Not having thumbs has brought so many opportunities for me to witness to people about my faith in God," she says.

Throughout her seventeen years of life, Amy has discovered there aren't many things she can't do. She's active in band, sports, serves on the youth council at her church and is president of Fellowship of Christian Athletes at her school.

What *can't* she do? Well, hitchhike, give a thumbs-up sign and do conventional sign language. But in tough times Amy, like Nann, has clung to her faith, her family and the Bible. Psalm 139 reveals that each person is "fearfully and wonderfully made," even with limitations.

What God will do with a willing heart is beyond our wildest dreams. It doesn't matter to him if that willing heart is inside a weak body; he's simply looking for obedient disciples.

SIX

Help!
My Friend Has Been Hurting Herself!

Dear Susie:

I have a problem I need help with. My friend has been extremely depressed. She told me she thinks she should be in pain, so she constantly cuts herself. She has gone to some doctors to find out why she's so depressed, but so far, they don't know.

She was doing better for a while, but now it's really bad. And she slept with her boyfriend, which I know doesn't help. She told me she has given up on God and doesn't want to get better, but I can tell she's screaming for someone to help.

I don't know what to do. I pray continually and have encouraged her and given her Bible verses, but I'm at the end of my rope.

Stacia

Imagine holding so much hurt on the *inside* that experiencing great physical pain on the *outside* would seem minor. Chava was fifteen years old when she started hurting herself. "I had really low self-esteem," she says, "and I was always condemning myself." In an effort to take her mind off the deep hurt she was harboring in her heart, Chava began cutting herself and burning her arms with a curling iron.

If you have a friend who is experimenting with self-mutilation, he or she may be known as a "cutter." It's dangerous, and your friend may be stuck with physical scars for a lifetime.

It's difficult to understand why someone would voluntarily inflict pain on herself, isn't it? No one simply begins cutting herself for the fun of it. It's painful. Someone who is involved in self-destructive habits is a friend who is hurting reallyreallyreally bad! Oftentimes, she is trying to cover up a painful experience from the past or is trying to call out for help.

What can you do to help? First, let me share a little more of Chava's story to help you better understand what your friend may be feeling.

Chava's pain happened right before she entered her teen years. "When I was eleven," she says, "my family moved to Israel. While on vacation at a beach, I was raped by a twenty-nine-year-old lifeguard."

She didn't tell anyone, because since he offered her a ride, and she voluntarily got in the car with him, she assumed the rape was her fault. And she was embarrassed.

"I didn't know what to do with all that hurt," she continues. "It just wouldn't go away. It kept growing and gnawing at my insides."

Despite the nightmare she experienced at the beach, Chava enjoyed living in another country and learning about a different culture. "My dad is a rabbi," she says, "and my family loved being in Israel."

But when she turned fifteen, her dad decided to move the family back to the United States. "I didn't want to come back," Chava explains. "I became very bitter about having to move again and having to move such a long distance. I was just getting used to the culture, the food, the climate and the people."

Trying to Fit In

When Chava arrived back in the States, she felt like an outsider. "I spent a lot of time trying to figure out where I fit in," she remembers. "All my friends had changed. It was really hard to find common ground with anyone, even with my best friends. They all thought I was weird."

Chava discovered one of her friends was bulimic. "I had always carried a phobia about my weight," she says, "and the fact that my one friend was bulimic influenced me to obsess about my own weight."

Because Chava was still hiding the pain from being raped, it didn't take long for her to attempt to fill the void in her life by controlling her weight. She began throwing up three times a day and finally got to the point where eating anything made her physically sick.

Her parents noticed the changes in their daughter and tried to help, but because Chava was determined to continue hiding her pain, they were limited in what they could do. They *did*, however, get her into counseling.

The Hurt Won't Go Away

Not only was she dealing with the secret of being raped, weight fluctuation and rejection from friends, Chava's grandpa shot himself and died a month after she had returned from Israel. "I saw him one day, and he died the next," she remembers.

"I didn't want to keep thinking about all the hurt inside me. I was desperate to get my mind off all the sadness and confusion I was feeling," she says. So one day at a friend's house, when Chava was fifteen, she took a sewing needle and scraped her hands and arms. "Later, I told my mom that my friend's cat had scratched me," she says.

"Part of me was thinking, *I can't believe I'm doing this.* But the other part of me was able to numb the pain on the *inside* because now I was focusing on a different pain—a physical pain on the *outside.*"

Is There Hope?

Chava was finally hospitalized because of excessive cutting and because of a suicide attempt. She was diagnosed with major depression and was placed in a lock-down facility. "I felt very far from God," she remembers. "I kept thinking, *He won't love me. Why would he? I'm too unworthy. I'm worth nothing.*"

But Chava's parents and church family continued to love her and pray for her. When she was released from the hospital, she began attending a weekly women's Bible study with her mom. "It was four hours long," she says. "We'd bring our workbooks and read out loud and really dig into the Scriptures."

Chava had loved dancing since she was a child, and one day the Bible study group was listening to some soft music during their prayer and worship time. "The song was 'El Shaddai,'" Chava remembers. "I've always loved that song. I felt God was touching me in a special way. During the next few minutes, I got up and danced the song for the women."

Afterward, the women surrounded Chava and prayed with her. "I gave God one hundred percent," she says. "I gave him everything! I can't go back to the hospital. I can't continue to self-destruct. I can't keep destroying the temple God has given me."

Is she still tempted? "I'll be honest," Chava says. "I still struggle with the temptation to cut myself. I'm still battling bulimia, but God is working with me. Some of my healing may take time, but he's not giving up on me. I've surrendered myself to his care, and with his help, I know I'll make it.

"I'm so much closer to my parents now," Chava says. "The biggest help they've given me is to make me realize they're not giving up on me. They hug me a lot. They smile with their eyes as well as their mouth, and they show me in a million ways that they love me.

"My parents bought me a journal and assured me that it was for all my private thoughts and that no one would ever read it unless I chose to share it. There's such a security in that. So, I'm writing down my thoughts now," she says. "That really clears my head. I love to write poetry.

"Later, I go back and reread what I've written and it helps me gain a clearer perspective of what I'm struggling with. I also try to listen to calming music. Some of my favorites are Twila Paris, Kim Hill, Nicole Nordeman and Point of Grace."

"Yup, I have a friend who sounds just like this girl. She has little scars all over her legs, where it doesn't show except in the locker room. But I just don't know what to say! Please help!"

I understand how concerned you must be. Here are some things to keep in mind when you're trying to help someone in this situation.

Don't:

- Condemn her. Your friend already knows what she's doing isn't right.
- Point attention to the physical scars. She knows they're disgusting. Remember those scars have come out of great pain. Your friend doesn't know how to accept herself. She hates who she is.

Do:

- Watch for warning signs: Wearing long shirts when it's not cold (to cover scars from cutting or burning), being overly modest (not wanting to change in front of people), wearing shorts and a shirt over a swim suit (so no one will see the scars).
- Ask your friend straight-out if she's cutting or burning herself.
- Give your friend lots of hugs. Pray for her often, that God would bring peace into her life.
- Encourage her to get professional help. Offer to go with her if she's afraid to go by herself. Check with your pastor for a list of Christian counselors to recommend. Remember, it's not simply a few cuts or burns. Your friend is trying to cover up something much worse.

Ask your friend if the two of you can get together at least once a week to read the Bible together. Ask God to speak words of love and affirmation to her through your reading. It's important to be praying for your friend. But also ask your friend if you can pray *with* her.

Encourage your friend to journal, like Chava is doing, or to release her pent-up anger through physical activity like jogging, slamming tennis balls against a backboard, biking or hitting a punching bag. Even though a punching bag will cost a few dollars, it'll be worth every penny spent to keep from hurting herself.

SEVEN

Help!
My Friend Has Been Sexually Abused!

Dear Susie:

My best friend, Janna, just told me an awful secret. It's so gross, I'm not sure it's true.

She said her stepbrother ... well ... abuses her. Sexually. I'm shocked. And my heart is breaking for her. Help!

Sherry

Sexual activity among family members is called **incest**, and it's the most common type of sexual abuse. Studies suggest that *one out of every four girls* is sexually abused by someone in her family. For boys, the figure is one out of seven.

Incest happens not only within *immediate* families but in *extended* families as well (between kids and their stepparents, grandparents, uncles, stepbrothers and so on).

Two Types of Abuse: Covert and Overt
Incest may be covert (concealed or less obvious) or overt (out in the open or blatant—something physical between two people).

- Jodie's uncle committed covert incest when he forced her to look at pornographic magazines.
- Anna's stepbrother committed covert incest when he took photos of her undressing.

- Tasha experienced overt incest when she was alone with her grandfather and he began touching her sexual organs.

Whether incest is covert or overt, it's still sexual abuse and is always a *crime*. Incest has been reported in every race of people in every era of time. If you have a friend who is a victim of incest, she's not alone. And neither is she at fault.

> *"Susie, someone who's being sexually abused might not say anything because she's too ashamed. How can you tell if someone is being sexually abused? Are there any signs to look for?"*

Good question! It's likely that one of your friends at school or in your church youth group is trapped in an incestuous environment. It's possible that a friend is being sexually abused if you observe these signs:

- She has low self-esteem.
- She has difficulty establishing proper relationships with the opposite sex (either completely withdrawn or promiscuous).
- She's into self-mutilation (cutting or burning herself).
- She reacts in a defensive manner when touched.
- There are dramatic changes in her school performance.
- She frequently complains of "general" pains.
- She has frequent mood swings (happy one minute, sad the next).
- She is severely depressed.

- She has eating problems. (Sexual abuse can lead to eating disorders, such as anorexia nervosa or bulimia. In fact, some researchers say that 80 percent of all eating disorders can be traced to sexual abuse.)
- She exhibits extreme hostility toward parents.
- She overreacts to common problems.
- She is fearful of basements, closets or dark spaces.
- She feels unworthy of God's love and forgiveness.
- She's often angry but directs her anger at the wrong person—maybe *you!*

Though some of the above characteristics can result from other problems, if you notice that a friend displays *several* of them, it may be a sign that she's being sexually abused.

If you think one of your friends is being abused, it's time to consider sharing your suspicions with a trusted adult. But don't act *too* quickly—nobody likes rumors and misinformation spread around about them. In fact, the reputations of honest and totally innocent parents and families have been ruined because of false rumors and gossip.

"So what's the first step?"

Get the facts first. Gently approach your friend and ask a few leading questions. Let her know you can be trusted. Remind her how much you care about her and value her friendship. She may not share her problem right away, but the important thing is that you stand by her, especially when she's angry or depressed.

Breaking the Silence

When your friend *does* decide to talk about her sexual abuse, realize that there's an immediate crisis the moment she tells you! Because you are now aware of the situation, things can never be the same again. By consciously choosing to share such a painful, personal part of her life with you, she is also choosing to break the conspiracy of silence.

It's important to realize that your friend has spent a long time building and maintaining a silent wall around this private area of her life. This intimate secret has been meticulously guarded. She will be very nervous about what you might do with this new information, so be extremely careful about how you proceed!

Try to express your concern in the following ways:

1. Thank her for sharing her secret with you. Gently explain that you're not equipped to handle such a huge problem, but that you'll help her in any way you can.

2. Pray with her. Remind her that God feels her pain. Memorize this verse together: "The Lord is close to the brokenhearted and saves those who are crushed in spirit" (Psalm 34:18).

3. Cry with her. If you genuinely feel like crying, there's no need to hold back. Sometimes tears say a lot more than words. Let her know you share her pain.

4. Listen, listen, listen. The healing process begins when the secret is revealed, and your friend may want to talk about her experiences and her pain. If so, practice good listening skills: focus your entire attention on her, don't interrupt, maintain eye contact. If your friend isn't comfortable opening up, don't push or pry. She'll talk when she's ready.

5. Help her sort through the confusion, but don't give advice. Your friend will probably be confused about a *lot* of things—her parents, her faith, her values and her feelings. For a while, she may feel that everything in her world is chaotic. YOU can be the one stable thing in her life, the one who points her to the Stabilizer, Jesus Christ. Still, be careful not to give unasked-for advice. Your job is to be a friend, not to try to fix everything.

6. Don't walk out on her. You may feel uncomfortable receiving such intimate and personal information. You might be embarrassed and nervous. That's all right—it's perfectly normal to feel that way. Whatever you do, though, don't ignore or avoid your friend or her problem. That would break her trust at the very time she needs it most.

For your friend, the hard stuff is just beginning. Remembering (or sharing) an abusive situation is like a puzzle falling into place *one piece at a time.* As the experiences and emotions come together, she'll need a tremendous amount of support! Plan on being involved in her life the next several months or years.

7. Point her toward qualified professionals. She may feel as though her whole life is a puzzle—but she'll also begin to realize that one important piece is missing. That piece is her childhood. She was robbed of a normal, healthy childhood. Like all of us who lose something important, she needs to grieve the loss. This means she needs a professional counselor to guide her through this process.

You are not equipped to help put her life back together. If you're a true friend, you'll help her find the right people to talk to.

8. Don't make promises you can't keep. In trying to comfort and console your friend, you may be tempted to make promises you won't be able to live up to. Do *not* promise that you won't tell anyone. If her situation is to ever get better, you *have* to tell someone eventually!

Don't promise you won't tell just because you're curious about her secret, or because you feel sorry for her. **This is not a secret for two teens to keep between themselves. A trusted adult *must* be brought into the situation or your friend will never get the help she needs and deserves.**

"So what do I say when my friend says to me, 'I need to tell you something, but you have to promise you'll never tell anyone!'?"

A good response would be: "I care about you very much, and I want to help. I can tell something's bothering you, and it must be pretty important for you to want me to make such a bold promise. But *because* I care, I can't make that promise. I will, however, promise to stand by you. THAT you can count on."

9. Be honest. While you don't want to make rash promises that you can't keep, you *do* want to offer honest comfort. Here are a few things you CAN say *after* she has shared her situation with you:

- "Because I care about you, I cannot let you continue to be abused."
- "Together, we need to decide how to get the help you need."
- "I will have to intervene."
- "I am not trained or qualified to handle this situation by myself. I want your permission to involve another person."

10. Be there. Your presence is far more important than having the right words to say or knowing exactly what to do. Sometimes there *aren't* any words that will comfort. Don't feel like you have to say just the right thing. Simply *be* with her. Be willing to sit right next to her in total silence for a couple of hours if that's what she needs. Your presence will speak volumes to your frightened, lonely friend.

Jill's Story

Jill works down the hall from me at Focus on the Family. She's an outgoing, beautiful young lady. You'd never guess that years of pain lie hidden behind her smile. Though she's never publicly shared the hurt she has experienced, she wants to offer hope to teen girls who may be trapped in an incestuous home. Therefore, she has decided to talk about her past right now. If you have a friend who's being sexually abused, please ask her to read this. Here's Jill's story.

My parents divorced when I was only six months old. My mom abandoned me because I reminded her of my dad. She said I was a fat, ugly baby and didn't want anything to do with me. So I ended up at my grandmother's house—with my mom's mother. That's who raised me.

My grandmother was perfect on the outside. She and Grandpa had lots of money and could always afford the most fashionable clothes and the best of everything. We all went to church every Sunday, smiling on the outside but falling apart on the inside. You see, Grandma was mentally ill and emotionally abusive.

She constantly said hurtful things to me, such as, "We buy you such pretty clothes, but they look so horrible on you. Too bad you're not a pretty girl."

And she played weird mind games with me. For instance, she'd point to a red book and ask, "Jill, what color is that?"

"It's red, Grandma," I'd say.

Then she'd start screaming and violently insist that it was blue. She'd point her finger at me and yell, "You're an idiot, Jill! You're so stupid!" This would go on and on until I'd finally give in and agree that it was blue.

You can imagine after *years* of this, I began to see the world around me in her abnormal way. I learned not to trust what *I* perceived as reality, but to accept *her* reality instead. Soon I began believing that I really *was* fat, useless and ugly.

Grandma was extremely controlling. She read all my letters and monitored all my phone calls. I had no privacy. My entire world revolved around whatever she wanted it to be.

When I was thirteen years old, my grandpa died, and it seemed as though something snapped inside my grandmother, making her even crazier. Her brother—my great-uncle—began coming around. She said it was because Uncle Mac wanted to represent a father figure to me.

He started picking me up after school and taking me to movies and fancy, four-star restaurants. One evening as we walked to his car, he cornered me between another car and a wall. I was shocked when he slid his hand up my shorts. I pushed him away and screamed, "What are you doing?"

But he grabbed me and pushed me against the car, pressing his body close to mine and rubbing himself against me. I felt dirty and ashamed. I began thinking it was all my fault. *I shouldn't have worn these shorts,* I thought. *I'm so stupid! I must have given him some kind of signal or something.*

Even though I blamed myself for what had happened, I knew that what he had done was wrong. I'm not sure *how* I knew; I just knew it.

When I got home, Grandma was standing at the kitchen sink, washing dishes. I told her exactly what had happened. She was furious! She pulled a wet plate out of the sink and hurled it at me while screaming, "You're a liar! You're a no-good liar, Jill!"

Then she locked me in my bedroom for two days. The only time I was allowed to come out was to use the bathroom. I received no food and no water. She said I wouldn't be released from my room until I admitted that I had lied.

Finally, I couldn't stand being a prisoner in my bedroom any longer. I gave in just to be able to eat and get dressed and walk around the house. She then called Uncle Mac and told him to come over because I had something to tell him.

I was then forced to apologize for what I had said. I had to tell him that I lied, and I had to agree to continue seeing him.

By the time I was in high school, I had developed bulimia. Oftentimes, eating disorders can be traced to abuse. I realized that my great-uncle had sexually abused me, but I didn't realize that I was being emotionally abused by Grandma. She was constantly telling me I was fat, stupid and worthless. I knew she was mentally ill, and it was obvious that she was mean and controlling, but I didn't know this was considered emotional abuse.

Controlling my food intake was one way that I could take charge. Subconsciously, I wanted to control my own life and my own body. No one else could dictate what I would eat or wouldn't eat. I wanted everything on the outside to look as perfect as possible in order to make up for how lousy I felt on the inside.

Right before my high school graduation, Grandma told me that she knew where my dad was. I hadn't been in contact with him at all, so you can imagine my surprise to learn his whereabouts! She allowed me to send him a graduation announcement. He attended the graduation and even treated me to dinner.

We really clicked. I loved being with him, and he seemed so sympathetic and understanding. He had learned—even through the short time he was married to my mom—what my grandma was like. I felt I had finally found an understanding friend. We promised to keep in touch after I got to college.

As I left for college, I was totally unprepared for living and relating in a normal world. It was hard for me to make good decisions. I had to depend a lot on what others told me, because I had spent years with an abusive relative pounding false reality into my brain.

I started dating a guy who was also emotionally abusive. Thinking back on it, maybe I was drawn to him because that's what I was used to. I found out later that he was a serial rapist on our campus. He stood in front of the dorms and studied the freshman girls going in and out. He watched them long enough that he could tell which ones struggled with low self-esteem. Naturally, I was an easy target.

He befriended me and started the relationship by showering me with kindness. But it wasn't too long before he began being extremely possessive. He isolated me until he was the only person I saw, and he began controlling my life. Again, since I was used to this from living with my grandma, it all seemed normal.

One night he called and canceled our date, so I went out to eat with a girlfriend. It just so happened that we spotted him at the same restaurant with another girl. I was furious! I told him I never wanted to see him again.

Later, he phoned me while drunk and began calling me every horrible name in the book. I held my ground, though, and said it was over. A couple of days passed, and he called again—asking if we could talk. I turned him down and repeated that we were finished.

A few hours later, I heard a knock on my door. I thought it was the girl down the hall returning some books I had loaned her. I opened the door and saw *him* instead.

He was extremely apologetic and nice, and even though I knew I shouldn't, I let him in. When he began talking about getting back together, I continued to stand my ground. "We can't," I said. "It's over. I don't want to go out with you anymore."

He became angry and started screaming at me, so I told

him to leave. "Then open the door and let me out!" he yelled.

I stepped past him to turn the doorknob, but as I did, he grabbed me from behind. He threw me down and raped me. I screamed, but no one could hear because he held a pillow over my face.

I reported it to the campus police, and they questioned him, but he had made up an alibi. He had some friends say that he was in his room the entire time.

Two days later, as I was coming out of a night class, he jumped out of the bushes and beat me up. He tore a muscle in my back and dislocated my vertebrae. I was in a wheelchair for six weeks.

"If you don't drop the charges," he threatened, "I'll kill you."

I knew he meant business, and I was scared to death! He began stalking me—no matter what time it was or where I was, he was there. After several weeks, I was such an emotional wreck that I dropped the charges.

When I went back to Grandma's house in June, I was really restless. I had tasted freedom while away at college, and I didn't like being in her emotionally unstable and controlling environment any longer. I was also still trying to get over the rape, and I just needed a friend.

A college pal who lived a couple of hours away invited me to come spend a week with her family. Grandma said I could go, and I excitedly packed enough clothes for seven days. *This is exactly what I need,* I thought. Then for some unknown reason, on the day I was supposed to leave, Grandma changed her mind.

"If you leave for a week, I'll make sure you leave for

good!" she snarled. She started throwing my belongings everywhere. I was so tired of all the violence in my life that I decided to go ahead and leave, even though I knew I would never have a home with her again.

I ended up coming back in two days, and my room was totally empty. All my possessions were gone! It was as if I had never existed. I told Dad what was going on, and he invited me to come stay with him and his wife.

Two weeks after I moved in with Dad, he started molesting me. It started with simple touching. He began touching me underneath my nightgown while saying, "You have nowhere else to go. I'm all you have. Just relax and go along with this, or you'll have nothing!" The abuse progressed from his touching me to him forcing me to touch him. From there, the abuse got worse and worse, until finally, he started having intercourse with me.

Eventually, I moved out of my dad's house, putting an end to the abuse, and finished my college degree. Breaking out of the abusive situation was the first step toward healing.

Putting the Pieces Back Together

The hopeful news I want to share with you is that the friend you're seeking to help *can* overcome an abusive background and find healing and wholeness! Jill's story doesn't end with the cycle of hurt and abuse. There's more!

All my life, I continued going to church, reading my Bible and depending on God's guidance to get me through the traumatic times. And you know? Even though life wasn't fair, God was always there. He provided the strength I needed to carry on despite the abuse, and he walked with me through the nightmares.

I began going to counseling a year ago, and I'm getting stronger every day. God is helping me heal, and I now know he can make something beautiful out of *anything!* Through counseling and with God's help, I'm putting myself back together again. I'm slowly learning that I can trust my own view of reality. I'm becoming one person—whole and free! The path to healing has, indeed, been long and difficult. But the good news is that there's hope for anyone who has been abused.

Counseling is often hard work. It's not easy to talk about the pain and hard times I've experienced. But healing is so important to me that sharing the hurt is worth it. There's no way I could do it without God. He gives me hope and fills my life with purpose and meaning.

I'm now thirty-three years old, and God has blessed me with a terrific Christian husband and two great children. It's taken a while, but I've finally learned that my self-worth doesn't come from what other people say about me. For years I thought I was no good because the people closest to me kept telling me how rotten I was.

I now know that my self-image comes from being uncon-ditionally loved and totally accepted by God. Can you imag-ine how free that makes me feel? I don't have to live in the past anymore! I don't have to dwell on trying to understand *why* this or that happened. I can simply relax and bask in his great, overflowing love for me.

What about you? Do you have a friend who has been sex-ually abused? Have *you* experienced sexual abuse? Though it may seem impossible, I want you to know that you CAN get your life back. You CAN become the young lady God intends for you to be. Please believe me—there IS life after abuse.

"Where can I call if my friend wants to get out of her abusive situation but has nowhere to go?"

Help *is* available. Your local phone book or toll free directory (800-555-1212) will have several hot line numbers listed on the inside front cover. Consider calling one of those numbers or one of the following:

- Abuse Registry
- Child Abuse/Family Violence
- Focus on the Family (ask for the counseling department) 1-800-232-6459
- Minirth Meier New Life Clinics

EIGHT

Help!
My Friend Was Forced to Have Sex!

Dear Susie:

The hottest guy in school asked me out. I was really excited, because every single girl is in love with him. He asked me to our football homecoming. After the game, we went to a party where alcohol was being served. I didn't really want to go, but I didn't know how to say no.

He started drinking and offered me a drink, too. I declined, but he kept pressuring me. Everyone else was drinking, so I finally gave in. I really didn't have that much, but I wish I hadn't taken any.

After about an hour, he suggested we leave. He drove me to a secluded area and started getting physical with me in the parked car. I was really uncomfortable. He'd had way too much to drink, and I kept telling him I didn't want to do this. But he only got more forceful.

I finally slapped him and pushed him off me, but that only made him angry. He forced me to have sex with him.

I feel so betrayed and hurt. I don't know what to do. If I tell my parents, I'll get in major trouble for drinking and for parking. Help!

Cyndi

What Cyndi has just described is date rape—sometimes it's called acquaintance rape. Sadly, these kinds of attacks are very common. It has been reported that 57 percent of all rapes happen on dates.

Every single hour of every single day, seventy-eight women are raped in the United States. That equals 1,872 rapes every day, 56,160 rapes every month and 683,280 rapes every year. (These are reported cases only. It has been estimated that only about 1 percent of all sexual assaults are reported to the police.) One out of three women will be sexually assaulted in her lifetime.

"What can I do to avoid being raped by a stranger?"

It's wise to take precautions. Here are a few tips to minimize your chances of you or your friends becoming victims of sexual assault.

- When shopping at the mall, always park your car near a light or as close to the building as possible. If someone follows you or approaches you as you are leaving—even to ask for help—alert mall security.
- Always carry mace spray (be sure you know how to use it) or a whistle with you in a place that's easily accessible.
- Avoid being alone in secluded areas (parking lot, jogging alone, hiking, etc.).
- Always lock the car doors when driving—even in daylight.
- Talk to your parents about getting a cell phone for the car, to be used *only* for safety reasons or mechanical emergencies.
- Listen to your senses. If you "feel" something's wrong, it very well could be. Leave the area immediately.

It's always a good idea to exercise caution and not take unnecessary risks. However, it's also important not to live in fear. The next time you feel afraid, here's a good verse to memorize:

> When you pass through the waters, **I will be with you;** and when you pass through the rivers, they will not sweep over you. When you walk through the fire, **you will not be burned;** the flames will not set you ablaze. **For I am the Lord, your God.**
>
> ISAIAH 43:2-3, emphasis mine

"It's hard to imagine anyone I know doing something like this to me. Do I really need to be concerned?"

It's good not to live in fear. However, it's a mistake to think that sexual assault (rape) could never happen to you or your friends. That's one of the most dangerous myths about date rape. Let's look at a few of these myths and dispel them with the truth, so you'll be better equipped to help a hurting friend.

Myth: "It would never happen to me."
Truth: Date rape (as well as rape) can happen to *anyone*. *No* one can be guaranteed absolute safety.

Myth: "It wouldn't happen to me, because I always know the guys I date."
Truth: Even guys you know can have a "night and day change" when they start drinking or if they are in emotionally or sexually charged situations.

Myth: "I wouldn't go out with anyone who would hurt me."

Truth: No one says to herself, "I think I'll go out with Ryan—he seems dangerous." You may not be able to see the danger signs in someone you know only casually. That's why it's important that you get to know the guys you date as friends first.

Myth: "I have great instincts. I'd be able to tell if a guy had that on his mind."

Truth: How can we tell what *anyone* has on his mind? None of us are mind readers! And our instincts aren't 100 percent correct all the time.

"Why would a guy force someone he knows to have sex? Lots of girls in my school will do it if they like the guy enough."

Date rape is *not* about passion or romance. It's about power, control and anger. You can't tell whether a person is capable of date rape simply by looking at him. He could be popular—a football captain or class president—or just an "average" guy. There are some characteristics, though, that many date rapists have in common. Here are some things to watch for:

- They begin having sex at an early age.
- They tend to talk about sex a great deal.
- They feel sex is an achievement, and it makes them feel important, powerful and in control.
- They are con artists who use only a moderate amount of force.

- They often have poor communication skills with the opposite sex.
- They are almost always into pornography, whether it's magazines, videos, the computer, music or all of the above.

How Do I Stay Safe?

"OK, this will help my friends and I know what danger signals to look for to know who not to date. Now, what are good ways to stay safe when we're on a date?"

Here are some tips to help you stay safe.

- Always trust your gut feelings. Our instincts aren't 100 percent right all the time, though, so it's better to err on the side of being too cautious than by being too trusting. If your date is making you feel uneasy, call it off. Or if the place he's taken you makes you uncomfortable, leave.
- Always stay completely away from alcohol and drugs.
- Always take money with you for an emergency phone call or taxi.
- Always stay in public places.
- Whenever possible, know not only the guys you go out with, but their friends and family as well.
- Never leave a party, game or concert with someone you just met or someone you don't know very well.
- Never continue to go out with a guy who puts you down.
- Never date guys who try to control you, your choice of friends or the way you dress.

"My friend Kelly is a mess. She's been
dating this guy Jason for a month.
This weekend they were making out,
and Jason wouldn't stop. She told him
no, but he just kept going. Kelly says it's
not rape because Jason was her
boyfriend, and she was kissing him.
What do you think?"

No means no. Even if it's a boyfriend. Even if there was kiss-ing involved. Date rape is never the victim's fault. Even if a woman's poor judgment has put her in a dangerous situation, no one has the right to violate her body even if they have become aroused. Using force to get farther sexually than your partner is willing to go is rape. No exceptions.

Anyone who has experienced date rape will have a confusing array of feelings—anger, fear, depression, humiliation and lack of trust in others. In cases like Kelly's, the victim may also try to blame herself:

- "I should have worn something different."
- "I must have given out some signals I wasn't aware of."
- "If only I would have been more careful."

It is perhaps because of this false sense of guilt that only 1 percent of all date rapes are ever reported to the police. Many times the victims will simply withdraw, or try to put the whole thing behind them. Neither of these approaches is helpful. Date rape is a serious crime. It's a betrayal of trust and leaves emotional scars that can never be forgotten or stuffed down inside. Sooner or later, your friend will have to deal with what has happened to her. It's best to start the healing process right away by bringing what has happened out in the open.

If you have a friend who is in this situation, you need to let her know that you are there for her and will stick with her. Remind your friend that when a girl says no, *no one* has the right to cross that boundary. Let her know over and over that if she said no and she's feeling guilty, she's feeling false guilt. Remind her that you love her and believe in her.

Encourage your friend to get professional help. Though you can give her tons of emotional support, you are not equipped to help her deal with the pain. Call your local rape crisis line for immediate help, and they'll help you get in touch with a professional therapist.

"What should I do if my friend comes home from a date and tells me her date forced her to have sex?"

Call the police. Your friend will also need to be examined by a physician—immediately. Don't let her shower, wash or change clothes. Valuable evidence could be destroyed.

Believe your friend. Give her as much comfort and support as you can. Go with her to the hospital, police station or counseling center. Keep repeating that she is not to blame!

"Why is it important to be examined by a doctor?"

Your friend needs to see a doctor because of the danger of sexually transmitted diseases (STDs) and the risk of pregnancy. She may be very embarrassed, and might not want to tell a police officer the details of her experience or to be seen by a doctor, but it really is in her best interests to do so. You can help by helping her tell her parents, staying with her and encouraging her.

"What if my friend doesn't want to involve the police? Does she have to press charges?"

The best help you can give her is getting her to report what happened. *Rape is a crime!* Your friend is a victim. As much as she would like simply to take a shower, throw her soiled clothes away and try to forget the nightmare, the smartest thing to do is to go immediately to the police. It may not be pleasant. She may feel like *she's* being interrogated. But it's important, for her own sake as well as for the sake of the rapist's future victims, that she try to put a stop to the man who violated her.

"Why do you think date rape has become so common in our culture?"

I believe there are several factors contributing to the increase in this type of crime. Here are a few of them.

1. *Increased portrayal of sexual violence in the media.* Our society is obsessed with sexualized violence. People flock to see movies with rape and violence. Think about some of the most popular movies being advertised.

2. *Increased availability and use of pornography.* Pornography reinforces the myth that women want sex even when they say no or if it's painful.

3. *Men are often taught that their masculinity is tied to their ability to be aggressive and to "score" sexually.* Unfortunately, this message is often reinforced by peers, especially when there is no strong father figure to show the young man a better way.

4. *Society's strong endorsement of drinking alcohol.* "You're not a real man unless you drink." Seventy-five percent of all date rapes involve alcohol or drugs. Think of all the beer commercials and how many of them target teen guys!

"My Friend, She's Fascinated With Sex ..."

Dear Susie:

My friend has confided something really personal to me: She's fascinated with having sex. She says she knows what she's doing is wrong, but every time she gets into a dating situation with a guy, she just can't resist.

She says she regrets it and tries to say no, but she always ends up giving in. I prayed with her, and she asked God to forgive her, but she always ends up falling back into her old routine. How can I help her resist this temptation?

April

I appreciate your deep concern for your friend. You asked how to help her resist temptation. Accountability will certainly help, but the Holy Spirit is the One who empowers us to say no.

I'm wondering if your friend was sexually abused in her younger years. Many times, girls who have that history, find it hard to say no in dating relationships. If she shares that with you, please encourage her to seek counseling. She may be equating sex with love.

I'm going to answer the rest of your question as if you're the friend you wrote about, OK? Then, hopefully, you can take what I've shared with you and pass it on.

You may already know this, but let me remind you anyway: The blood of Christ is more than enough to cleanse you from every sin and mistake. When you surrender your life to Jesus, God makes you completely pure and spotless. "Therefore, if anyone is in Christ, he is a new creation; the old has gone, the new has come!" (2 Corinthians 5:17) And check out what 1 John 1:9 says: "If we confess our sins, he is faithful and just and will forgive us our sins and purify us from all unrighteousness."

Even though his forgiveness is exciting, it's not a free ticket to deliberately continue sinning (see Romans 6:1-2). True repentance means an attitude change that eventually shows up in your lifestyle. In other words, it means, "I don't intend to do that ever again!"

This doesn't mean you'll never be tempted again. You may always be tempted in the area of sexual activity. But that doesn't mean you have to give in. You see, this is where the Holy Spirit comes in. Once we decide to live in radical obedience to the lordship of Jesus Christ—totally surrendered to his will and not our own—we don't control our lives any longer. We give up control to God.

Galatians 2:20 talks about dying with Christ. In other words, we decide to give up our rights, our wants, our plans— just as Jesus did—to follow God's way. If you continue to give in to sexual temptation, you're not allowing God to have ownership of your life.

Check this out: "No temptation has seized you except what is common to man. And God is faithful; he will not let you be tempted beyond what you can bear" (1 Corinthians 10:13).

Here's another great verse to grab hold of: "Because he himself suffered when he was tempted, he is able to help those who are being tempted" (Hebrews 2:18).

Please find some good Christian friends, or an adult you trust, who can remind you of Scriptures like these when times get tough.

One more thing: Premarital sex *does* leave emotional scars in your life. This doesn't mean that you'll never have a good relationship with the opposite sex, but you definitely need to establish some accountability and strong boundaries in your life.

Sex is an incredible gift from God himself. I encourage you to claim secondary virginity and to remain sexually pure from now until you share wedding vows with a godly man for a lifetime of Christ-centered marriage.

What You Can Do to Avoid Date Rape

Obviously, you can't stop date rape from happening. But you *can* encourage your friends to set high standards for themselves and be an example by setting high standards *for yourself.* Here are my suggestions:

Date only Christians. I realize that anyone can say he's a Christian, and that sometimes Christian guys are more "handsy" than nonbelievers. But set a high standard for your dates. Decide now to date only solid Christian guys. If you're not sure about his spiritual status, don't go out with him.

"But what if there aren't any Christian guys where I live?"

It's possible that you may not get to date until you're in college. You may not date until you're out of college. It's OK. You won't fold up and die. I promise. Take advantage of this time to deepen your relationship with Christ. (And turn to chapter twelve to find out other stuff to keep you busy in the meantime. Don't worry ... you're not alone!)

Know the guy well. And don't settle for simply knowing *him.* What's his family like? What church do they attend? How does he treat his parents? His brothers and sisters?

Date someone with similar values. If you don't go to dances, why date someone who does? Try to date guys who won't question your standards, but guys who will respect them and help you maintain those standards.

Pray about your dating relationships. This is the most important thing you can do! And even though it might feel weird, I hope you'll also begin praying right *now* for your husband. I realize you don't even have a clue who that will be yet, but go ahead and start praying for him. In fact, let's do it right now, OK?

Dear Jesus,

Thanks for the man you have selected for me. I don't want anything less than your choice for my life-time mate. Help me to be patient and to wait on your timing. Father, whoever he is ... be close to him right now. Help him to grow strong in you. Give him good Christian friends who will encourage his relationship with you.

Help him to establish high standards and to maintain them. Strengthen him, Father. Help him not to yield to temptation. Keep him pure.

Help him begin developing **now** into the godly man I'll need some-day. And help **me** to begin developing into the godly woman **he'll** someday need. Keep me pure, Jesus, I trust you with my future and with all my relationships.

Amen.

Help!
My Friend Thinks She's Pregnant!

Dear Susie:

Todd and I had been dating for seven months. He told me he loved me, and I believed him. I loved him, too. We started sleeping together when his parents weren't home. I never thought it would happen to me, but ... now I'm pregnant.

I'm not very far along. In fact, I'm not even showing yet. But I bought one of those pregnancy tests from the store, and it showed that I'm pregnant.

I told Todd, and he dumped me. He said I should have been more careful—that I should have been taking something.

I can't believe this! I'm only sixteen years old. I'm on the volleyball team at school. I feel like my life is over! I can't tell my parents. They're Christians, and they'd die. Please help me!
Courtney

What To Do

First things first. When your friend shares this kind of secret with you the best thing you can do is pray with her at that very moment. Choosing to participate in sex outside of marriage is a sin. She needs to repent and seek God's forgiveness. And the exciting thing about our heavenly Father is the fact that he *will* forgive her! She can start all over.

Though there will be consequences that she'll need to deal with, she can still live a victorious and joyful life in Christ. You can help her realize that by praying with her and by listening to her pray.

"Does my friend need to tell her parents?"

Though she may not want to tell her folks, encourage her to do so. They really need to be a part of the next nine months *with* her. They may or may not be supportive, but they still need to know.

After she has told her parents, hopefully they'll begin to guide and help her with the medical attention she'll need. If, by chance, they disown her or refuse to help her, *you* step up to the plate and prove what friendship is all about.

"But I don't have a lot of money. How can I help her get the medical care and other things she needs?"

If she can't afford to see her family physician, take her to the county health department. It's important that she get medical attention early, because:

1. The health of the baby is at stake and
2. Her health is at stake (she needs to be examined for STDs).

Your local crisis pregnancy center can be an extremely valuable place to turn to! You can find them in the Yellow Pages of the phone directory. They're experienced volunteers and can help your friend with decisions she'll need to make.

"Should she tell the father?" Definitely! He has a right to know.

"What if he denies being the father?" You could suggest he take a blood test, but why push it? If he's in denial, he has some major problems. You know the truth! And so does God!

"Should they get married for the sake of the baby?" No. There are thousands of people who would be thrilled to adopt, love and care for this little one.

"My friend's parents are really mad, and they want her to have an abortion. What should she do?" I sincerely hope your friend won't even consider abortion as an option. I believe abortion is murder. If your friend does not have the support she needs to take care of the baby herself, encourage your friend to consider putting the baby up for adoption. There are thousands of childless couples waiting in line to receive a newborn. Many times these couples will help the birth mother with her expenses to get her through her pregnancy. Call your local pregnancy counseling center for more information. And don't forget to call out to your Heavenly Father for help in time of need:

Hear my cry, O God;
    listen to my prayer.
From the ends of the earth I call to you,
    I call as my heart grows faint;

lead me to the rock that is higher than I.
For you have been my refuge,
    a strong tower against the foe.
I long to dwell in your tent forever
    and take refuge in the shelter of your wings.

PSALM 61:1-4

If Your Friend Starts Dating Again

Chances are, in time your friend will become involved in another dating relationship. You can help your friend not repeat the same mistake by encouraging her to establish firm boundaries for herself and holding her accountable to those boundaries.

- Date only Christian guys.
- Don't spend prolonged time alone with him.
- Strive to group date as much as possible.
- Stay in public areas such as miniature golf, bowling, tennis, shopping, etc.
- Have a plan before the date actually begins: Know where you're going and how much time it will take. This way, you won't have two extra hours at the end of your date with nothing to do. That's what gets many teens in trouble. Then stick with the plan.

Many teen girls feel there must be something "wrong" with them if they're not dating anyone. In fact, just today, I received a letter from a girl saying, "Susie, no guy has ever asked me out. I'm already fourteen. What gives? Is there something wrong with me?"

Let me share with *you* the same thing I told her, OK? Why assume if you don't have a boyfriend that something must be wrong? That's ridiculous! Many girls don't date until college or later. Your confidence, fulfillment, happiness and security *must* come from a deep, intimate, growing relationship with Jesus Christ—not a guy.

Please understand—and help your friend understand—that we serve a God BIG enough to send just the right guy into your life at just the right time—according to his will. (Memorize Habakkuk 2:3 from the Living Bible, OK?) By keeping your focus on *God* instead of obsessing over guys—you'll keep dating and sex in the right perspective: Dating in God's time, and sex only with your husband after your wedding ceremony.

help!
my friend thinks he (or she) is gay!

Dear Susie:

I'm a sixteen-year-old, pasta-loving, energetic, all-out-for-Jesus gal, but I'm concerned about a friend of mine, Jeremy. Last winter, he decided he is a homosexual because he's not attracted to girls.

He doesn't **want** to be gay, and he's prayed for God to heal him, but he's still not attracted to females. He recently decided to stop crying and being depressed and simply accept his homosexual feelings. But the good news is that he's open to talking about this, and he wants help. What should I do?

Cassandra

If you have a friend like Jeremy, there are some very important ways that you can be Jesus to him (or her). The very best things you can do for your gay friend are:

- Continue to love your friend.
- Continue to encourage him or her to seek Christian counseling.
- Ask if you can pray together once a week.

Sure, it would be easier just to go your separate ways. You may find your association uncomfortable at times. But at some point, your gay friend's world *will* fall apart. As a Christian, I hope you'll be the bridge he'll need that leads back to the church. If you simply turn your back on him, who will be that bridge?

Dear Susie:

This is my first year in public school, so I was glad to find a morning prayer group. But there were some things about Chase, our student leader, that made me uncomfortable. He was always hugging us and telling everyone how God had ordained him to preach.

Then I found out that Chase is bisexual. And no, it's not a rumor. I left the prayer group. Some of my friends still go, and I don't know how to tell them about Chase without gossiping.

I don't know him well enough to confront him about it, even though the Bible says to confront a brother one-on-one if he's in sin.

In a school where Christians are already viewed critically, I think some kids think being gay is OK now. After all, Chase is gay and he's the leader of the prayer group. What should I do?

Katrina

I'm sorry this has happened, and I can understand why you feel uncomfortable. I encourage you first of all to turn to the Lord in prayer. He cares about every single detail of your life, and this situation is certainly no exception. You can tell God everything you're thinking and feeling, and then trust him to work things out in his time and in his way.

Sounds like Chase is very confused. We have a "Gender Specialists" department here at Focus on the Family that ministers to thousands of teenagers and young adults who are deceived into believing they're gay or bisexual. The folks who head up this great department are men who have come out of the gay lifestyle, and they'll all tell you that the homosexual lifestyle is a lie from Satan.

Satan would love to continue deceiving Chase and cause him to doubt his masculinity. Satan is using a void in Chase's life to confuse him about his sexuality. Of course, you can't tell Chase that. You've already said that you don't know him well enough to confront him. But you *can* continue to be kind to him. Smile and say hi to him when you pass him in the hall.

Maybe you can tell him privately that you appreciate his leadership skills in the Bible club, but you're not comfortable with his lifestyle and the fact that he's condoning it to others. Let him know you'll continue praying for the group, but you'll be watching only from a distance. That way, he won't wonder why you've suddenly dropped out.

Will you also consider sharing this with your parents and another Christian adult you trust, such as your youth leader, Sunday school teacher or pastor? One reason God has put these people into your life is to help you with situations like the one you're facing. They may have had similar experiences when they were your age. They may also have some valuable insight to share, and they could pray with you about this, too.

Helping Someone Who Struggles With Same-Sex Attraction

I personally believe that homosexuality is a lie from Satan. I'm not saying people don't struggle with an attraction to the same sex. I *am* saying that I believe Satan is the Father of Lies and loves to deceive folks into believing they were born gay and

144 / Help! My Friend's In Trouble!

there's absolutely nothing they can do about it.

Check the statistics: most gay men will admit they had a less than solid or even nonexistent relationship with their father. Every single boy in the world needs love and attention from a male figure. God put that desire within him, and that's why his perfect plan includes two parents for each family.

When a boy doesn't get the love and nurturing from his father that he needs, he finds himself yearning for intimacy with other males. He often assumes, "I must be gay, because I want to be close to a man. I want to be hugged and touched by him."

Most guys who grow up with a healthy male role model who gives them the attention and touch they need (wrestling with them on the floor, hugging, playing sports with them, etc.), don't feel a need to be drawn to members of their own sex. That need for male bonding has already been met.

So what am I saying? I believe that many people who are involved in homosexual relationships *think* they're gay, but they're not—they're simply yearning for something they never received growing up. Satan takes this need—twisting it and perverting it into something against God's will.

"Lots of Christians I know do everything possible to avoid contact with homosexuals. Some of my friends think that if you're friends with someone who's gay, you're condoning his or her lifestyle. What do you think?"

As Christians, we need to treat the gay community with love and respect. Jesus never qualified his love, did he? He never said, "Clean up your act, and I'll love you." We have no record in Scripture of Jesus saying, "Quit living in sin, become who I want you to be and I'll accept you."

Jesus loved everyone, especially sinners. That's the entire reason he left the glory and splendor of heaven! He wants to intimately invade our lives with love, meaning, purpose, forgiveness and wholeness. He expects us to treat sinners the same way he does—with much love.

Now, here's the tricky part: Jesus loved, but he didn't condone. We are commanded to love everyone, but we are *not* to accept a sinful lifestyle. Jesus never made excuses for people's sin. He never said, "Well, that's OK. I know you're confused. Go ahead and sin. I'll stick with you. We'll eventually work it out."

Jesus allowed people to feel guilty for their sin, he forgave them and he led them into a changed lifestyle. We can do the same. As the church (the body of Christ), it's our responsibility to make the gay community feel welcome—just as we would an unwed, pregnant teen mother; or someone with a jail sentence, or an ex-robber. We need to welcome *everyone* into the church and love them to Christ.

But there *is* a fine line in welcoming and loving ... and accepting a lifestyle of sin. We can accept the person without accepting the lifestyle. Wrong is wrong. Sin is sin. And what God calls sin will *always* be sin. We can love those who are gay, yet let them know that we don't accept their lifestyle.

Practically speaking, how do we do this? One of the best examples of this can be found in the Gospel of John, chapter eight. Remember the story of the woman caught in adultery?

Read it again—and let's compare the behavior of Jesus (who loved the woman but hated her sin) and the Pharisees.

The Pharisees:

- Labeled her and talked about her as though she were not a real person. *"The Law of Moses commanded us to stone such women"* (John 8:5).
- Exposed her to further their agendas (to trap Jesus) rather than to help her (8:6).
- Condemned her without considering whether they, too, might have hidden sin in their own lives (John 8:9).
- Their intent? To bring her *death*.

Jesus:

- Prayed for wisdom (as he wrote in the sand) before speaking (John 8:6-7).
- Spoke to her personally, privately, and with compassion (John 8:10-11).
- Focused on the present and the future rather than the past (John 8:11).
- His intent? To bring her *life*.

As you interact with those struggling with homosexual feelings, always remember that we are to try to be more like Jesus! If you are unsure of how to handle a particular situation, please talk with an adult whom you trust spiritually—your parents, pastor, youth leader, etc. God has placed these people in your life to guide you, and they'll probably have some valuable insight you can use.

Guess What?

When you love your gay friends yet refuse to accept their lifestyle, you'll probably get a lot of flack. But that's how Jesus lived his life, and that's how he expects us to live ours—in imitation of him (see Ephesians 5:1).

"But I thought as Christians we're supposed to accept everyone. I have non-Christian friends who are living in sin. I can't just dump them. And I'm not sure God would want me to."

Good point. Glad you jumped in. Before we wrap up this chapter, let's just chat about that, OK? Just between us (as in you ... and me).

God commands us to love *everyone*. In fact, love is one way the world can see that we're different. "A new command I give you: Love one another. As I have loved you, so you must love one another. All men will know that you are my disciples if you love one another" (John 13:34-35).

And get this: "Dear children, let us not love with words or tongue but with actions and in truth" (1 John 3:18).

Here's one worth memorizing: "If anyone says, 'I love God,' yet hates his brother, he is a liar. For anyone who does not love his brother, whom he has seen, cannot love God, whom he has not seen. And he has given us this command: Whoever loves God must also love his brother" (1 John 4:20-21).

"So, what's it mean? If we're supposed to love everyone, how can you come on so strong against stuff?"

While God calls us to love everyone—including sinners—He never asks us to love a sinful lifestyle. In other words, He wants us to love the sinner and hate the sin.

"But as Christians, aren't we supposed to be tolerant?"

You're right—to a point. We're to be tolerant in
- not demanding to be first
- not always assuming our opinions are right (notice I said *opinions*—which is different from what's written in the Bible)
- listening to those around us
- accepting everyone—regardless of race, belief or physical attributes
- allowing others to express their views

In these areas, tolerance is definitely a virtue (meaning, a real good thing; a characteristic to be desired.) But tolerance isn't *always* a virtue!

Let's look at our example: Jesus loved everyone, but he didn't tolerate sin. Remember when he chased the money changers out of the temple? Another time, he got so angry at sin, he cursed a fig tree, and it withered. *Some* folks who claimed to be godly people were called hypocrites by him!

See, tolerance doesn't mean accepting everything. It *does* mean accepting people—but as sold-out disciples committed to his lordship—we have to draw the line at accepting (or being tolerant of) sin.

Tolerance applies only to persons, never to truth! Tolerance applies to the erring; intolerance to the error. We must be tolerant with people but *intolerant* where truth is at stake. We can't afford to compromise what the Bible says is wrong and become tolerant of those who rationalize it as right. Sin is *always* sin. Anytime you hear someone say, "Well, maybe it's wrong for me, but I can't say it's wrong for someone else," you're listening to dangerous rhetoric.

Again, sin is sin. What the Bible says is wrong for *me*, is also wrong for *you*.

"But when we put it that way, doesn't it make us sound judgmental?"

Yeah, it probably does. But sometimes it's OK to judge. Let's sneak a peek at what the apostle Paul has to say about it:

> When I wrote to you before I said not to mix with evil people. But when I said that I wasn't talking about unbelievers who live in sexual sin, or are greedy cheats and thieves and idol worshipers. For you can't live in this world without being with people like that. What I mean was that you are not to keep company with anyone who claims to be a

brother Christian but indulges in sexual sins, or is greedy, or is a swindler, or worships idols, or is a drunkard, or abusive. Don't even eat lunch with such a person.

It isn't our job to judge outsiders. But it certainly is our job to judge and deal strongly with those who are members of the church, and who are sinning in these ways.

1 CORINTHIANS 5:9-12 TLB

In other words, it's *always* OK to call sin "sin." It's OK to be intolerant of sin. We don't have to accept it—we're not *supposed to* accept it. Paul encourages us not to hang out with people who *say* they're Christians but don't abide by God's Truth.

When it comes to sin and truth and the compromising of God's Holy Word, it's OK to be narrow-minded. After all ... we're walking a straight and narrow road.

For more information or help, contact:

Exodus: Christian organization that provides materials and counseling for teens involved in the homosexual lifestyle. (206) 784-7799

Restoration: Christian ministry to homosexuals who desire a lifestyle change and to Christians who struggle with homosexual feelings. (970) 663-7778

"It's No Big Deal, God, But ..."

Hatred stirs up **dissension** but love covers over all wrongs.

PROVERBS 10:12

ELEVEN

Help!
My Friend's a Hypocrite!

D ear Susie:

One of my friends listens to Korn but preaches about how she's going to save herself until she's married. It makes me mad because it's unfair. I don't listen to it, and I'm saving myself too. She's a cafeteria Christian—picking around at various churches for a friendlier religion. What can I do to help?

Tori

The beginning point in witnessing to an unbeliever is a consistent and sincere expression of unconditional love and respect. Don't get into arguments with her. You may win a battle but eventually lose the war.

Your lifestyle shouts volumes! Ask God to give you opportunities to gently share his truth with her. He knows exactly what your friend needs to hear. While you'd probably love to hurry the whole thing up and get her "right with Christ" immediately, remember that God's timing is perfect. She may not come to know him overnight, but let's trust God that she'll eventually give herself 100 percent to his authority.

Meanwhile, since she's into Korn, how about offering her some Christian music that has a close sound? Most Christian bookstores now have listening centers so you can actually hear a CD before you purchase it. Ask the clerk to help you find similar sounds for your friend.

And about her virginity: I hope she *does* wait until marriage. It sounds as though you're frustrated because she's being hypocritical—saying she'll save herself for her husband—but at the same time filling her ears with music that blasts all kinds of sexual perversion. Yes, that *is* hypocritical.

But remember, anyone can say no to sexual intercourse. That doesn't make someone a Christian. Philippians 3:18 tells us that many who call themselves Christians are really enemies of the cross. And we're told in 1 Timothy 3 that it's not easy to live a godly life.

We learn in 2 Timothy 3:1 that it's going to be really tough to be a Christian in the last days. The Bible also describes your friend's desire to be a "cafeteria Christian"—picking and choosing what she wants to believe. The New Testament warns us that in the last days people in the church won't want to hear the truth. They'll become upset at good, holiness preaching, because it will make them uncomfortable. So they'll leave that church and go to another, hoping to hear something that will tickle their ears.

Your friend is confused right now, but the good news is that she's searching. Keep loving her—even when you want to scream at her—and trust Christ to give you continued opportunities to share his love and truth with her.

When a Friend Gossips

A gossip betrays a confidence, but a **trustworthy** man keeps a secret.

PROVERBS 11:13, emphasis mine

He who **guards** his **lips** guards his **soul,** but he who speaks rashly will come to ruin.

PROVERBS 13:3, emphasis mine

Dear Susie:

My best friend and I had a huge blowout. She's been mad at me for a whole month now. And ... I'm pretty ticked off at her, too. She let something slip that I shared with her in confidence. That really hurt! I'm afraid our friendship is damaged forever.

Jacki

Your friendship doesn't *have* to be damaged forever. It's up to you. Will you decide to forgive and forget? I realize you've been terribly hurt, but you've probably let things slip before, too. No one's perfect—not you and not even your best friend.

I always think it's sad when two good friends let a misunderstanding come between them. Be bigger than the problem, Jacki. There's only one Person who can help heal the hurt inside you and give you the ability to forgive: Jesus Christ. Wanna talk with him about it right now?

God Said ... I Said

This is a private conversation. DON'T READ ...
unless you enjoy eavesdropping.

God said: You miss her, don't you?

I Said: Alison?

Yes.

Ah, not really.

Hmmm. Not even walking to school together?

Nah. It's kind of nice being alone. Gives me time to think.

Not even having lunch together in the school cafeteria?

It's probably better that I eat faster anyway; it gives me time to leave and get started on my homework.

And what about youth group?

Well, I'm still going to Sunday school. I guess it's not that important that I go to youth group all the time. I wouldn't want to go and be there with Alison. It would feel too awkward.

Isn't it awkward *now*—holding this grudge against her?

Well ... yeah ... things are weird. But ... it would be even *weirder* to forgive her.

Or would it?

Huh?

Just how long do you plan on trying to avoid her? Eating alone. Hanging out by yourself. Missing youth group. Wouldn't it be easier to simply forgive her and get on with your life?

No.

Are you sure?

Positive.

Hmmm. Remember the time you lied to your mom about breaking your curfew?

That was over a year ago! You sure have a good memory.

I'm God. I know everything.

Oh, yeah. OK, so what's the deal? Why are you suddenly changing the subject from Alison to my curfew? That has absolutely nothing to do with how she hurt me.

The point is, you lied. But I forgave you.

Well, that wasn't hard to forgive. It was only curfew!

My child, any time you lie, you're being deceptive—and that goes directly against my holy character. It hurts me.

Hurts you? Nah. Murder—that hurts you. And children starving. That's gotta hurt. And your heart probably breaks every time someone is abused. But stretching the truth about curfew? Nah, that can't hurt.

When you lie, my child, you're breaking one of the Ten Commandments. You're going directly against my plan for your life. You're sinning. Every sin—murder, abuse, stealing, gossiping, lying—they *all* hurt me. And they hurt deeply. I *died* so that you wouldn't have to pay the penalty for those sins.

I'm sorry, Jesus. I guess I just wasn't thinking that stretching the truth about my curfew was really a sin. But, you're right. *Any* time I choose to deceive someone, I'm lying. I'm so sorry.

I know you are. I know your heart. It's tender. I have forgiven you.

Whew! That sure feels good.

But we're not finished.

Well, yeah we are. You know I'm sorry. And I've accepted your forgiveness.

But we're still not finished. What about Alison?

Oh, man! Why did you have to bring *her* up again?

Because she's my child, and I love her deeply. I died for her, too, you know.

But, God! She really hurt me. She *really* hurt me! I mean ... You have no idea.

Oh, I know all about hurt. Two of my own disciples betrayed me. One sold me for a lousy thirty pieces of silver. My *life* for thirty pieces of silver! And the other one— one whom I had nicknamed "The Rock" and said I'd build my church on—lied and said he didn't know me—had never even heard of me. Yes, my child, I know all about hurt.

Yeah, but Judas was a weirdo from the very beginning. Alison's not a weirdo. What I'm going through doesn't even compare to a couple of disciples—especially since Peter got back on good terms with you—and Judas was such a flake.

Flake? Weirdo? The day before I selected my twelve disciples, I had spent the entire night praying about whom to choose. None of them were chosen flippantly. Judas was chosen to follow me, because he was full of talent and ability. He showed promise and possessed such an eagerness. He wasn't weird. He was good with numbers. He was dependable. The other disciples trusted him enough to put him in charge of our financial funds. Yes, he eventually betrayed me, but it didn't happen overnight. He slowly began backing away emotionally and spiritually before he

ever made his physical move of betrayal. I know about hurt.

Yeah, but it all turned out OK.

OK?

Well, yeah. I mean, he killed himself. So you never had to think about it again. I'm always running into Alison, and the hurt is fresh every time I see her!

My heart broke for Judas. If only he would have sought me out before hanging himself. If only he would have found me.

Why? What difference would that have made?

A lot. You see, My child, I would have forgiven him—if only he would have asked.

Forgiven him? *Forgiven him?* He betrayed you! How could you have forgiven him?

He's not the only one who has betrayed me.

Well, yeah ... Peter. But he sought forgiveness.

Peter and Judas aren't the ones I'm thinking of right now.

Well, who else, God?

You, my child.

Me?!?

You.

Please don't say that! I'd never betray you.

When you refuse to forgive someone who has hurt you, you're betraying me.

No!

I want you to forgive Alison.

I can't, God! It hurts too much!

I understand. I know all about hurt. And when *you* hurt, I hurt. I've cried the tears with you. You've never been alone.

But, God, it's just not fair! She promised she'd never tell anyone. I trusted her. I wouldn't tell just *anyone* who I like. And she gave me her word she'd never tell. Then she had to go and blab it to Justin that I think he's hot. How could she? I've never been so embarrassed in my entire life!

I understand. I created you, and I know how badly your heart is bruised right now. But, I promise ... it's not the end of the world.

It sure feels like it!

And even though Alison broke a promise, she never really betrayed you.

What?!?

She was trying to get Justin to ask you to the cookout next week.

What?!?

She thought if he knew you liked him, he'd have the confidence he needed to ask you.

What?!?

It's true.

Well ... what ... she ... I mean ... how ...

She *did* break a promise—and I know you're hurting over that. And she *did* tell Justin something that you're wishing he didn't know. But she didn't do it out of spite. Believe it or not, she was trying to help. Granted, she didn't think it through. Yes, she should have talked it over with you—

asked your permission. But she wasn't out to hurt you. That was not her motive.

I never knew.

Because you never asked.

She should have told me.

She tried. But it's hard to hear when you're running away while she's talking.

Well ... I didn't know.

You reacted out of hurt, instead of expecting the best in her.

It still hurts.

I know.

And I'm still embarrassed.

I realize that. But if I can forgive those who have wronged *me*, shouldn't you also forgive those who break your trust?

Yeah, probably.

Could you be a little more definite?

But I'm still angry! And I don't think it's fair that I should have to forgive her. After all, she *did* promise. She broke her promise, God!

And I know your hurt. But the bottom line is this: You'll break one of your promises to me sometime in the next couple of weeks. Should I forgive you?

Well, sure, God! You know my heart. You know I love you. And yeah, sometimes I blow it, but my relationship with you is important to me. I always ask you for forgiveness when I know I've gone against your will.

My child ... if you don't forgive those who hurt you, it

stands in the way of *my* bestowing forgiveness upon *you.*

But, God! You can't hold this against me! Alison hurt me.

And you'll hurt *me.*

You've gotta forgive me when I blow it. I'm just sixteen! I don't always realize I'm even *doing* something that hurts you until I'm right in the middle of doing it. But I'm always sorry!

I know you are. I know your heart.

Okay, then.

But I also know Alison's heart. And I know that she's sorry about the embarrassment she's caused you. She loves you. She treasures your friendship. You two have a lot of great memories together. I want you to forgive her. By extending your forgiveness to her, it keeps your heart uncluttered and allows my forgiveness to flow freely to *you.*

Wow. I never thought of it that way before. It's really pretty complicated, isn't it?

No, not really.

Well, it *sounds* complicated.

It's simply a decision to allow me to be Lord of your life. Not just your future, your talents, your family. But allowing me to forgive others through you—letting me be the Lord of your hurt, too.

I think I'm getting it, God. But I still don't think it's fair. I mean, she *did* hurt me!

Forgiveness isn't always fair, my child. But it's always right.

And sometimes it hurts to do the right thing.

You *are* getting it!

Well, to be honest ... I *am* pretty tired of carrying this grudge around. I really miss my friendship with Alison. I think I'll go call her. I'm gonna need a ride to youth group tonight.

And you're also going to need a ride for Saturday.

Saturday?

That barbecue. The cookout at church.

Nah. I don't think I wanna go. I'd be too uncomfortable around Justin.

First dates usually *are* a little uncomfortable.

First dates?

Justin.

You mean—

Yes.

Oh, my goodness! I'd better run to the mall. I don't have anything to wear! I've gotta get moving! I'll buy those khakis I saw marked down half-price, and I might be able to get—

I wouldn't go just yet.

Why not?

Because before you'll even have time to get to the mall, your phone will be ringing.

Justin?!?! How do you know? I mean, how can you—

Trust me. I'm God.

You're right. I'll sit right here, God. I'll stay right next to the phone, and I won't pick it up until he calls.

No. Go ahead and pick it up. There's someone *you* need to call, remember? She needs your forgiveness.

Oh, yeah. And maybe there's something else I should give her.

Yes?

A huge apology.

You really *are* getting it, aren't you?

Well ... I *do* have a great Teacher.

I love you, my child.

Thanks. And God?

Yes?

Thanks, too, for being patient enough to keep on with me until I finally get it.

TWELVE

Help!
I've Never Had a Date!

Dear Susie:

I'm sixteen years old, and I've never had a date. The problem is I **want** to. I'm scared I'll never marry, or no one will ever like me. It's kind of embarrassing. Some of my friends are two or three years younger and have already had many boyfriends. I just want one—someone really special. I'm not shy or quiet, and I have lots of friends that are guys, too. Help!

Brandi

I know several girls reading this have a friend who feels exactly the same way you do. It's tough that your younger friends have already had many boyfriends, but what does that prove? Only that they've had their heart broken and have had to deal with the frustration of rejection, and you haven't!

I get lots of mail from girls your age who think there must be something wrong with them simply because they don't have a boyfriend yet. What's the hurry? If everyone else put dirty socks on a chain and started wearing them around their neck, would you? I hope not!

Brandi, I wish you were here right now. I'd love to treat you to some ice cream and give you a big hug. Know what I'd tell you? "You're completely normal!"

Repeat after me: "I'm completely normal!" Say it again: "I'm completely normal!"

Brandi, many girls don't date until college, and other girls don't have a boyfriend until they're out of college and into a career. Please realize it's not a *guy* that gives meaning to your life—that can come only from a solid, growing relationship with your Creator.

It's totally normal to want a relationship with a guy. God created that desire within you. But it will happen in his perfect timing. He's never early, yet he's never late.

Can I challenge you to do something? Will you memorize this verse? I'm going to give it to you from the Living Bible, because I like the way this particular version states it. Here it is:

> But these things I plan won't happen right away. Slowly, steadily, surely, the time approaches when the vision will be fulfilled. If it seems slow, do not despair, for these things will surely come to pass. Just be patient! They will not be overdue a single day!
>
> HABAKKUK 2:3

Hey, Brandi, there *are* a few advantages of not being tied down to having a boyfriend right now. Don't believe me? OK, I'll give you ninety-nine. You've gotta come up with the hundredth one on your own, OK? Here goes:

1. When you're ready for a new 'do, you don't have to worry about cutting off too much hair. (Why do guys like long hair anyway?)
2. You're more open to trying new things when you're flying solo. Try guitar lessons, sign up for a pottery class, join a Bible study.

3. There's more time for others when you're not sold out on one guy. Hang out with your family, visit people in nursing homes, shovel snow off your neighbor's driveway.

4. You can eat an artichoke and onion pizza and not have to worry about impressing anyone with your breath.

5. Concentration exists. Your mind is completely clued in to your homework, your weekend job, your chores and most important (drum roll, please)—your relationship with God!

6. You can wear your favorite pair of platforms as much as you want! Who cares if you're taller than all the guys in your class?

7. When you're not in Coupleville, it's easier to avoid stuff God would never be too thrilled with—like feelings of jealousy and lust.

8. You can rent chick flicks as often as you want.

9. No worrying about what to give him on his birthday, Christmas and anniversaries.

10. No worrying about whether his buds like you.

11. No worrying about whether his parents like you.

12. Basically, just fewer worries.

13. God's timing is always perfect. It really, truly is! And if you need proof, check out Habakkuk 2:3.

14. If you ever held back in Foosball, Ping-Pong or pool just to make a guy feel good, you don't have to anymore. Let your full potential soar!

15. There's more time to take a jog, hit the gym or walk your dog around the block.

16. Got a zit on your forehead? Who cares?

17. You've got lots more opportunities to hang out with the ultimate guy in your life—Jesus!

18. No special boy means no special breakups. You get to avoid the crazy roller coaster so many others have gotten a bit queasy on.

19. Everybody knows you as *you*, not so-and-so's other half.

20. When you're happy being single, you're able to set high standards for the kind of guy you'd like to go out with someday.

21. You can cry without being accused of PMS.

22. You don't have to have "the talk" about where your relationship is heading.

23. Building lots of good relationships with girls and guys is way more healthy than spending every waking second with one particular person.

24. No more sitting by the phone. You've got better things to do with your time.

25. Your room's a lot less cluttered. There just aren't as many things to save when a guy's not around.

26. You're into the courtship thing.

27. Hitting the mall with your girlfriends is tons better than with a guy 'cause they're more likely to understand why it takes you forever to decide between lilac and sky blue nail polish.

28. You can let your creative juices flow and put together a totally outrageous outfit without having to wonder what he'll think about it.

29. Telling the truth is much easier. Without a guy you'll never hear yourself say anything like, "Yeah, I live for monster trucks," "I'd love to go hunting with you this

weekend," or "Sure, the corner convenience store sounds like a great place to eat."

30. You've got your whole life ahead of you. Why rush into things? Just 'cause every other girl you know has a boyfriend? Come on! Who really wants to be just like everybody else, anyway?

31. The dough you would have spent on little gifts for him can go toward something more important—such as little gifts for your sponsored child in Ethiopia.

32. Maybe your parents have said, "No boyfriends for you, young lady." If so, no problem. Obedience is a *good* thing!

33. You know, sometimes boys have a not-so-great smell.

34. You've always loved fairy tales, nursery rhymes and limericks? Now you can write your own children's book! What are you waiting for? Get cranking!

35. The Diet Coke is all yours now. (And his backwash is long gone.)

36. You have plenty of opportunities to catch up on some bonding time with your mom or sister or long-lost friend from camp.

37. No gal-pals from his past to deal with.

38. Rebecca St. James, Margaret Becker, Jaci Velasquez, Kathy Troccoli and me ... all of us are single women fulfilled in our relationship with Christ. If we can be secure without a guy, you can too!

39. Your friends don't get antsy when you're taking a long time to get ready for an evening of fun.

40. Instead of listening to his band play at the local coffee shop, you and the girls can start your own band!

41. No more badgering your friends to find out if they really like him!

42. You finally have a chance to fill your diary with stuff other than *him*—you know, dreams, goals, answers to prayer.

43. You can spend Friday evening with a bowl of popcorn, a bottle of Snapple and *The Princess Bride* and not have to worry about him being bored.

44. No more looking at *Field and Stream* magazine—unless you really *want* to.

45. Bored without a boyfriend? No need to be! Try creating your own board game. Hey, it was probably a woman without a guy who created "Candy Land" and "Sorry!"

46. It's way cool to be able to check the oil in your car all by yourself.

47. You now have some spare moments to pull out the sewing machine and make that too-cool skirt and top you've had your eye on.

48. Hey, you could even design your own pattern!

49. No more straining to read between the lines to figure out what he's really saying.

50. Finally! You've got an opportunity to really get involved in church. Consider helping out in the nursery, teaching the kindergarten Sunday school class or visiting a senior citizen who hasn't been able to attend in a while.

51. You get to spend Monday nights watching "7th Heaven."

52. Every single day of spring break can be spent with the

girls, and you don't have to feel guilty about leaving him out.

53. No stressing about where things will go after high school. You can confidently head off to the college of your choice!

54. When you hear a girl in the hallway talking about her disastrous relationship, you can lend a caring ear and feel grateful that you're not in her situation.

55. No need to revolve your summer plans around him— God's got big plans for you! Hey, maybe you'll head overseas on a life-changing missions adventure!

56. Don't wanna wash your hair today? Then don't!

57. No need to explain why a brownie topped with chocolate ice cream, doused in chocolate chips and hot fudge, served with a cup of hot chocolate is a great lunch.

58. You can listen to all your fave girl bands without having to switch to his music picks.

59. You're not spending time with someone simply because you feel guilty about saying no to his relentless offers to take you out to dinner.

60. Yahoo! You can hum the tune that keeps floating around in your head without feeling self-conscious.

61. You don't have to rack your brain trying to come up with a bunch of conversation starters to get him talking.

62. And those long awkward silences are now a thing of the past. (Maybe only a temporary thing of the past, but still, be glad that you're not having to work your way around them at this point in time!)

63. You can throw yourself into doing more around the house. Why not gather up all the stuff no one uses anymore and have a giant garage sale? Then use the moolah to do something nice for someone else.

64. When you ace trig, make the honor roll *and* start on the girls' varsity b-ball team, there's no wondering whether he's intimidated by your accomplishments.

65. You can finish your steak *and* eat your loaded baked potato without worrying if you-know-who thinks you're eating too much.

66. Now that your mind's not all caught up in coupledom, you can play around in the kitchen with your friends. Why not create your own brand-new recipe for mouth-watering chocolate chip cookies?

67. When you're having major cramps, you can go ahead and scream or withdraw and not make excuses.

68. Think of the variety of photographs you can surround yourself with! Life's kinda boring when you've got the same face staring at you from your dresser, your bedside table, your closet door *and* your bathroom mirror.

69. You can wear your favorite navy sweater two Friday nights in a row without having a guy say, "Hey, isn't that what you wore last weekend?"

70. There are more available hours for you to spend baby-sitting, which means you'll have more money of your own—to put toward your car, your college education or your summer missions trip.

71. Have you been to the library lately? There are rows and rows of books there that'll pique your interest and send your mind and imagination into the lives of people from past and present. Find out more about other cool

single women such as Amy Carmichael and Corrie ten Boom.

72. There's no need to leave your house any sooner than necessary to get to school or youth group. You don't have to pick up any carless boys.

73. Your cat's a lot happier now that no one's picking it up by its tail.

74. Church, school, hockey games, dc Talk concerts, thrift stores ... at this point in life, who really has time for one guy?

75. You're free to wear the jacket of your choice without feeling like you should be wearing his.

76. The fridge and cupboards at your house are more likely to stay well-stocked since they aren't raided every day after school by someone who could eat you out of house and home.

77. You have absolute, total control of the TV remote!

78. Goodbye to being grilled by friends, parents, youth workers, etc. about every second you spent with a certain XY-chromosomed person.

79. When you're at a school activity, you're completely free to hang with more than one guy.

80. You've got more room in your locker than either of the attached girls with lockers next to yours.

81. There are enough things in life to say no to without having to deal with a guy who's pressuring you to get a little more personal than you want.

82. You have to bother with makeup only when you really want to.

83. You've been wanting to redecorate your room? Now's your chance.

84. You can start your Christmas shopping early! Hey, in one month all the winter stuff will be 60 percent off!

85. Without anyone asking you out, there's no chance of being stood up.

86. Your girlfriends will probably like you more now. This is a good time to maintain the friendships you might be ignoring if you had a steady guy.

87. No more having to share half of your Twix. You can eat both candy bars yourself. (Two for me. None for you.)

88. You don't have to deal with someone who's jealous when you're friendly with other guys.

89. Remember how your dad insisted that your last guy take his baseball cap off at the dinner table? You can certainly do without going through that again!

90. You'll probably have fewer all-around mortifying moments since you're not spending time with someone you really want to impress.

91. It's highly possible that you'll get more out of your youth group if you're not attached at the hip to a significant other. You'll probably hang with more people and focus better on your youth pastor's talks.

92. You can finally check out that part-time job you've been dying to get.

93. Have you always wanted to try your hand at watercolor? Get out the paints and go for it!

94. Now you have time to memorize 2 Corinthians 4:8-9.

95. After you've memorized the above Scripture, you've got time to get some adhesive paper and create your own bumper sticker based on this verse.

96. When something cracks you up, like a great joke or a hilarious movie scene, you can laugh so hard that you snort and not have to be embarrassed about it.

97. Tired of the same ol' same ol' TV sitcoms? Why not create your own?

98. You won't have to hear your friends say, "Are you talking about *him* again?"

99. Nothing's more attractive than a confident single gal who truly loves Jesus and feels secure in who he's created her to be.

100. _____

_____

_____

_____

OK, now it's your turn. Think of one more reason, and jot it here in the space provided. And again, don't be fooled into thinking that having a boyfriend will validate you. Only God can do that.

Dear Susie:

I saw an old guy friend of mine recently, and we've started talking and hanging out together. I want to be his friend—and I enjoy his friendship—but I don't think I'm ready for the "boyfriend—girlfriend" scene yet. I just don't think he'll understand, and I'm not sure how to tell him.

He's not a Christian, either. A little voice inside me is saying go with the flow, and another voice is telling me to hold back. I'm so confused! What should I do?

Becca

I admire your honesty and your tender heart. I'm also proud of you for wanting to take things slowly. This guy might *not* understand about simply being friends. But you'll never know until you talk about it.

There's another issue that I'd like to chat with you about, though. And that's the fact that he's not a Christian. That "little voice" inside of you that's causing you to be cautious is the Holy Spirit. God uses his Spirit within us to guide us in the way he wants us to go.

The tug you're feeling to "go with the flow" is a normal human desire—but it's a desire of the flesh, not of the Spirit. I believe God desires that we establish our strongest friendships with other Christians.

Am I saying not to befriend nonbelievers? Absolutely not! How will they ever see Jesus in our lives if we don't reach out to them? But there's a difference in reaching out and being friendly, and in establishing an intimate relationship.

My advice? You're eventually going to have to talk this out with him. Express your desire to remain friends and save your dating relationships for guys who share your faith and values.

THIRTEEN

Help!
My Friends Think I'm a Mooch!

Dear Susie:
My best friend told me that I'm a mooch. I don't think I am.
I really want to be a great friend. What do **you** think?

Hillary

Since I don't know you personally, I can't make that call. But if she's really your best friend, I'm guessing she's probably trying to help you. Sometimes it's tough to tell our friends what they need to hear.

Examine yourself. *Are* you a mooch? Do you borrow a lot of things from several different people and take your time returning those items?

Maybe this will help you determine if your friend is on track or not:

Who, Me—a Mooch?
Find out if you're the one who always wants a handout!
by Anne Williman

Constantly borrowing things from friends and family without paying them back? You may be a mooch! You know, someone who freeloads off others so much that everyone grimaces when she appears. Take this quiz to see if you qualify as mooch material.

178 / Help! My Friend's In Trouble!

1. The afternoon of the bowling party, all your favorite shirts are in the dirty clothes hamper. Your sister's got a new WWJD T-shirt, but she's at work. You

  a. call her at her job, begging to borrow it. If she says forget it, you dig out the Audio Adrenaline shirt you wore only half a day last Thursday.

  b. take her T-shirt. She probably won't notice it's gone. If she does, you'll make it up to her sometime in the next decade.

  c. ask your mother if it's cool for you to wear your sister's shirt. Then if your sister has a problem with it, she can take it up with Mom.

2. While at a Chinese restaurant with your friend, you have only enough cash to pay for the sweet and sour chicken dish that you absolutely love. But an egg roll sounds great, too. You

  a. plead with your friend to spring for an egg roll. What's a couple of bucks between best friends?

  b. promise to invite your friend to dinner the next time your older brother's home from college. The only cost to her? One egg roll.

  c. choose a cheaper dinner so you can squeeze out enough for the tasty egg roll.

3. Your friend wants her new dc Talk CD back, but you're not sure where you stashed it. You

  a. destroy your room as you look for it. If unsuccessful, you forfeit the water park outing with your youth group and use the money to replace your friend's CD.

  b. get an unlisted phone number and start wearing a wig to school. That way your now ex-friend will never find you.

c. level with your friend about the CD being lost. But you tell her when it turns up, she'll get it pronto. Meanwhile, you let her borrow your Supertones CD.

4. At the open house of the new crisis pregnancy center, a bucket is passed for donations. You

a. take a long drink of punch just as it comes your way—hoping it'll be passed around you.

b. dig out a couple of bucks from your jeans pocket. You were going to use the cash to repay Dad for yesterday's loan at Dairy Queen, but he'd support this cause, and you can repay him anytime.

c. pass the bucket without making a contribution, but ask for an envelope with the center's address on it. After you baby-sit next weekend, you can send a gift.

5. To prepare for the Solo and Ensemble Contest, you need private flute lessons. A woman at church offers to give you lessons if you'll help her out by watching her kids. You

a. talk with your mom about a fair exchange rate for her lessons and your baby-sitting. Then you keep careful records of when and how long the two of you swapped services.

b. decide to take her offer and show up for all of your flute lessons, but flake out a few times when she needs a sitter.

c. present your dad with his favorite candy bar, and then beg him to finance the lessons so you won't have to baby-sit.

6. Mom's fourteen-karat gold chain looks perfect with the mauve sweater you're wearing to the movies. You decide to borrow the chain. Once you're in the theater, you notice it's broken and fallen into your lap. You

a. jet out of the theater and hit the nearest discount store for a cheap imitation. Your mother will never know the difference.

b. call your older brother and ask if he'll take you to get it fixed. He'll have to spring for the cost of the repair, but you'll promise to do his chores for the next six months.

c. plan to tell your mom how sorry you are and offer to save your money to pay for the repair.

7. *Some girls from church are planning to buy a birthday present for your friend Angie. "Chip in any amount," they tell you. "Most people give about $5." You*

a. fork over five bucks and offer to wrap the gift after it has been purchased.

b. plead with the friend next to you to drop in a dollar on your behalf since you left your purse at home. You promise to repay her as soon as you can, which may be a while since you're low on cash.

c. remember that Angie didn't get you anything last Christmas and decide to throw in a couple of dollars for her gift.

8. *Your Sunday school class is having a potluck after church tomorrow. You*

a. beg Mom to bake her delicious three-layer chocolate brownies. She doesn't have much to do today, and you're going to the mall with friends.

b. grab a bag of generic BBQ potato chips on the way to church. Hey, they said to bring one dish, and those chips *will* fill a bowl. (OK, maybe a small one!)

c. slip Mom a five to buy ingredients for taco salad at the

grocery store. Once she's home with the goods, you get started on your creation for the potluck.

SCORING:

Question 1. a=2 . . . . b=0 . . . . c=1
Question 2. a=0 . . . . b=1 . . . . c=2
Question 3. a=2 . . . . b=0 . . . . c=1
Question 4. a=0 . . . . b=1 . . . . c=2
Question 5. a=2 . . . . b=0 . . . . c=1
Question 6. a=0 . . . . b=1 . . . . c=2
Question 7. a=2 . . . . b=0 . . . . c=1
Question 8. a=0 . . . . b=1 . . . . c=2

Add up your points. _____

12-16 points: Congrats! Mooching isn't a significant problem for you. You appreciate it when someone does something for you, and you make every effort to pay him or her back.

8-11 points: You tend to expect others to do for you without having to give them anything in return. Before you alienate friends or family members with this kind of attitude, ask God to help you become more sensitive about when you're mooching. Then work to improve.

Below 8 points: You *do* have room for improvement! But don't fret! The Lord can help you turn around and become more focused on meeting others' needs. Ask him to help you identify when and from whom you mooch. When you blow it with someone, apologize and do something nice for him or her. It'll take some work on your part, but pretty soon you'll see people smile when you enter the room!

FOURTEEN

Help!
My Friend's Into Goth Culture!

Dear Susie:

I'm really worried about my friend, Ryan. He only wears black clothing and he's totally into the Gothic scene. I realize that it's not a sin to wear a specific color, but there's something different about him. He's not his old self. He's getting weird. I don't understand this whole goth thing at all, and I'm scared for him.

Samantha

You're right—it's not a sin to wear the color black, but it sounds like Ryan is into more than simply color-coordinating his wardrobe.

There's a college student at my church who used to be in the Goth movement. I've asked him to share his story in order to help you understand the movement a little better.

From Gothic To Godly
*Ever wonder if you can fill life's void
with something other than God?
Here's one guy who tried. And failed.*

When fifteen-year-old Erin left junior high and headed to high school, he struggled with the transition. With extra time on his hands during the summer, he became a big fan of the movie *The*

184 / Help! My Friend's In Trouble!

Crow. He also found new musical interest in Nine Inch Nails.

"I bought every single one of their albums," Erin says. "Trent Reznor became my idol. It was like I began turning into a Nine Inch Nails and Crow disciple. I was very insecure and didn't like myself at all."

Through His Ears to His Face

It didn't take too long before Erin decided that simply listening to the music wasn't enough. He began to dress in an all-black Gothic style and wear makeup.

"I used basic white on my face to make myself look really pale," Erin says. "I wanted to look sick and deathly. Then I'd use black to outline my eyes and lips, and paint my thumbnails and pinkie nails black.

"I became obsessed with death," he continues, "and I wouldn't wear anything but black. I grew my hair really long and even dyed it black to be like in *The Crow.*"

Erin began making daily trips to the cemetery and taking naps among the tombstones. He eventually got into vampiric stuff, but still felt a huge emptiness inside his heart.

"I didn't like myself," he says. "I was trying to become a different person, trying to find fulfillment. I even became sexually involved with my girlfriend." When he was eighteen, Erin moved with his girlfriend from Colorado to Tennessee to live together near her family. "But you know what? I still wasn't whole. Something was missing," he says.

And Then It Happened

"One day while on a farm in Tennessee, I was swinging an aluminum baseball bat against a tree," Erin says. "It ricocheted back and hit my cheekbone, splitting my skin and cracking my tooth. I immediately dropped to my knees and began praying.

'I need Your help, Jesus,' I said. I was scared and knew the Lord had been trying to get my attention."

Erin says God used that experience to wake him up spiritually. He witnessed to his girlfriend, but she wouldn't listen. Even though it meant leaving his girlfriend behind in Tennessee, he called his mom and explained that he wanted to come home. She sent him an airline ticket, and he was soon back in Colorado.

New Life

"When I came home," he says, "God started changing my life. I lost my obsession with sex and cemeteries, and wearing all-black clothing and makeup. The music didn't even interest me anymore. It's like I started seeing it through God's eyes, and it all began to disgust me."

As Erin gave control of his life to Jesus Christ, he also began to see *himself* in a new light. "I now like who I am," he says. "I'm a child of God, Erin Crow, not a Nine Inch Nails wannabe. I've been made in God's image."

And has that changed his dating habits? "I've asked God to forgive me for being sexually active outside of marriage," Erin says. "I'm so grateful he not only forgives me but also gives me a brand-new start. I'm claiming spiritual virginity. I know that physically I can't undo what I'd done, but I can commit to sexual purity and remain a spiritual virgin until I get married. I'm determined not to go beyond hand-holding and maybe a hug with any girl I date. In fact, I've decided not to even kiss a girl until I'm married to her."

Erin says that his former girlfriend got her own wake-up call about a year after he left Tennessee. She was badly injured in a car wreck and gave her life to Christ while recovering in the hospital. Today she's a committed Christian, too.

"But can't someone just dress Gothic and not really get messed up?"

"There's a lot of New Age stuff mixed in with the whole Goth culture," Erin says. "In fact, if you go back far enough, you'll find there are actually satanic roots in this movement. Witchcraft is also prevalent in Gothic culture.

"When someone simply dresses the part, it's called kindergarten gothic. But here's the danger: When you step into something, you always get more involved in it if you're actually doing it day by day. True Gothic is a lifestyle. It changes the way you live and talk—everything!"

"But I'm not looking to get involved in Goth culture or anything. I just want to be different!"

"It's a downward spiral," Erin warns. "It doesn't take long for Satan to get such a grasp on your life that you don't know what to do. I mean, I was contemplating suicide. For the teen who says, 'I just wanna wear the clothes and do the makeup,' he's kidding himself. It's a lie. Satan will use it to damage him."

Final Thoughts

Erin's favorite verse is John 10:10: "The thief comes only to steal and kill and destroy; I have come that they may have life, and have it to the full."

"That's what happens through the gothic culture," he says. "Satan uses it to destroy you and to steal your identity."

Erin is now plugged into church and is attending a Christian college. "I really have to watch the music I listen to. It has a big effect on me. I pretty much limit my music to Christian stuff," he says.

Even though God has forgiven him, Erin still faces the consequences of sin. "I struggle with thoughts about my past," he says. "I'm continually giving it to God over and over again. I want him to consistently be Lord of my life. I sometimes struggle with truly praising God and forgetting who's around me. I don't want other people's opinions to hold me back from worship."

Erin's advice to teens who want to deepen their relationship with Christ? "Don't settle for simply reading the Bible—study it. Since Jesus has completely changed my life and truly set me free, I now have an intense desire to win people to the Lord. He's given me such a hunger for his Word. I want to know it well enough to give answers to those who believe false teachings."

* * *

I hope you'll feel comfortable enough to share Erin's story with your friend Ryan. Don't stop hanging around him simply because he's frightening you. Assure him there's nothing he can wear that will cause you to stop being his friend. At the same time, though, let him know you're uncomfortable with the changes you see happening in his life.

FIFTEEN

Help!
My Friend's Afraid Violence Will Break Out At Our School!

Dear Susie:

My best friend, Allison, is really scared about all the violence that's happening in schools today. I want to help her, but I'm not sure how. I'm a little scared, too, but not like Allison. She thinks about the possibility of getting shot at school almost every single day.

Kristi

Unfortunately, many schools *have* become frightening places because of all the shootings that have been happening. Fear is a normal human reaction, but God doesn't want us to *live* in fear. He is the Author of Peace, and he wants you and your friends to bask in that peace.

A friend of mine wrote an article that we printed in *Brio* magazine that covers this very subject. I'll pop it in right here, so you can show it to Allison, OK?

You've Got What It Takes
No need to fear—Christ is here!
by Marty McCormack

With the start of another season that sends you off to public or private school, have you found yourself thinking that home-schooling sounds better and better all the time? Even if you love to learn, love to see your friends every day, love to stay after hours for sports practice or band rehearsal, you may be one of many with an uneasiness about just being *in* a school building.

So much violence has occurred in schools across the United States in recent years that young people from kindergarten to twelfth grade are apprehensive about being in a classroom where evil seems to reign. But you know what? If you're a Christian, you have Christ and the Holy Spirit dwelling inside you. That means through Christ, you've got the power, you've got the strength, you've got what it takes to go to school without fear.

Check out these verses from the Bible:

- "I will remain in the world no longer, but they are still in the world, and I am coming to you. Holy Father, protect them by the **power** of your name—the name you gave me—so that they may be one as we are one" (John 17:11, emphasis added).

- "I thank Christ Jesus our Lord, who has given me **strength,** that he considered me faithful, appoint me to his service" (1 Timothy 1:12, emphasis added).

- "But even if you should suffer for what is right, you are
blessed. **'Do not fear** what they fear; do not be frightened'"
(1 Peter 3:14, emphasis added).

A Healthy Perspective

Bad things are going to happen; and Jesus tells us that we'll
have trouble in this world (see John 16:33). People are going
to sin; God knows the state of our hearts (see Genesis 8:21).
Evil men will sometimes prosper; yet we serve a God who's in
complete control of everything (see Proverbs 11:21). Nothing
escapes him. Nothing surprises him. He knows what's going to
happen, and he knows how he's going to respond.

The question is, how do *you* respond when you see bad
things happening, people sinning and evil progressing? Here
are some courses of action to take you through the murky
waters.

No. 1: Be Joyful, Pray and Give Thanks
God clearly spells out his will for us—the way he wants us to
behave—in all situations: "Be joyful always; pray continually;
give thanks in all circumstances, for this is God's will for you in
Christ Jesus" (1 Thessalonians 5:16-18).

It's not easy to be joyful when everything around us looks
gloomy. It's not easy to pray when we don't understand what
God's doing. It's not easy to give thanks when something's
been done against us. But God tells us *it is his will* for us to be
joyful, to pray and give thanks. When we allow the Holy Spirit
to guide us in these things through the tough times, we'll be
one step closer to responding to evil in a way that pleases God.

No. 2: Recall God's Promises

The Bible records many promises God has given us. Take time to study the Word daily and try to memorize the promises of God. Then, when you find yourself in a difficult situation, God will be able to comfort you with his promises as he brings them to mind. Here are some to start with: Deuteronomy 31:6; Matthew 10:18-20; Philippians 4:19.

No. 3: Be Holy

We all have a contribution to make to society. Some choose to delight in perverse and evil things. A child of God will, by the guidance of the Holy Spirit, choose to live righteously. "For it is written: 'Be holy, because I am holy'" (1 Peter 1:16).

So how do we live holy lives? Paul wrote: "Finally, brothers, whatever is true, whatever is noble, whatever is right, whatever is pure, whatever is lovely, whatever is admirable—if anything is excellent or praiseworthy—think about such things" (Philippians 4:8).

What we think often shows up in how we act. As your desire for things that are good increases, you're likely to want to distance yourself from video games, movies, TV shows and music that glorify evil things. Examine your life and ask God to show you what evil influences you need to turn away from, and do your part to add good to our world.

No. 4: Live the Life

If you're professing a faith in Jesus Christ as your Savior with your lips, hopefully it also will be demonstrated in your actions. When everything around you seems to be falling apart, remember the rock your faith is built on. Don't doubt. Don't waver. God is your God, and he will give you all that you need to remain firm in your faith. "Now it is God who makes both us and you stand firm in Christ" (2 Corinthians 1:21).

No. 5: Trust

Jesus said, "Do not let your hearts be troubled. Trust in God; trust also in me" (John 14:1). If there's anything we can do in the midst of evil, it's trust in God. He's been around for all that's ever happened. Every death, every war, every sneaky attack Satan's made. And God's still around. We sometimes wonder what he's doing. We don't always understand his tactics. We question how he'll possibly be able to redeem a horrible situation. But he does it every day. God is always working for good. We need to always be trusting him to do that.

A Real Opportunity

So now that you're back in school, trying to live your life for God, why don't you participate in the annual "See You at the Pole" event? On a specific day in September, every year, millions of students around the world will gather at their campus flagpoles to pray for their schools, their countries and the world. You can play an important role in combating evil just by standing side by side with other students and lifting up a prayer to your heavenly Father.

Tell your school administration what you plan to do and then publicize the time and place for prayer. Many students will be meeting at their local time of 7 A.M. "See You at the Pole" is not a demonstration. It's completely legal. Check out the "See You at the Pole" Website at www.syatp.com for answers to your questions.

And remember: Be courageous! God commands it (see Joshua 1:5-9). Great and mighty is the power of God within you—much more powerful than anything else in the world!

* * *

Dear Susie:

I hear a lot about the "Last Days" and Christians being persecuted in other countries, but I've never thought a lot about it. I have a friend, though, who is really frightened about all this. She says she's afraid God is going to ask her to go through persecution some day.

She's a strong Christian, and I admire her relationship with the Lord. But it's weird hearing her say this stuff. It makes me uncomfortable.

Sarah

The Bible *does* say that in the last days Christians will be persecuted for their faith. Many people believe we're in the last days right now. Christians in Sudan, Africa and other parts of the world are definitely under persecution. In some countries, Christians can be killed for even meeting together. In Sudan, if your Christianity is discovered, you can be thrown in a refugee camp, beaten and tortured, and your children can be sold as slaves.

We have it a lot easier in North America, don't we? Still, I get letters from teen girls who are made fun of at school, home or at their part-time jobs because of their faith in Christ.

No one can say whether your friend really *will* be persecuted for her religious beliefs. It could be that she's simply frightened because of all that she's seen on the news. But it could also be that God is preparing her heart and mind for something that you and I don't know about.

Remember the violent killing spree at Columbine High School in Littleton, Colorado? Seventeen-year-old Cassie

Bernall was certainly persecuted for her faith.

It's been awhile since that's been on the news. Let me refresh your memory, with an article we printed in *Brio* magazine, OK?

Remembering Columbine
by Marty McCormack

Jesus said, "I am the gate; whoever enters through me will be saved. He will come in and go out, and find pasture. The thief comes only to steal and kill and destroy; I have come that they may have life, and have it to the full" (John 10:9-10).

One by one, we're all going to stand before the gate. Those who proclaim Jesus as their Savior will know the gate and enter through Him to find eternal life. Others who choose an alternate way will be on a path that only leads to death.

The twelve students and one teacher who were killed at Columbine High School in Littleton, Colorado, stood before that gate. They didn't know their turn to die would come so soon, but there was little they could do to prevent it. All they *could* do was be prepared.

Of the Christians who entered through the gate on April 20, 1999, seventeen-year-old Cassie Bernall was a current *Brio* reader, and seventeen-year-old Rachel Scott was a former *Brio* reader.

Cassie Bernall
The story of Cassie's life and death has made its way around the globe, and the last moments of her life have become a testimony to all who have heard of her boldness. She's been called a martyr because she was killed immediately after declaring her

faith in God. But Cassie was more than a martyr. She was a daughter, a sister, a friend, a student and a child of God.

"There was a quiet side to Cassie, but also a real fun-loving side," says her pastor, George Kirsten of West Bowles Community Church. "She had a name for different people. I think she called my thirteen-year-old son, who's kind of gregarious, a tree frog or tree monkey. Cassie was also a thinker. She liked to get into deeper conversations, and she talked a lot about her walk with Christ—not only with the kids at church, but also with the kids at school."

Cassie made it a priority to be involved with her youth group and spent Tuesday evenings meeting with a discipleship group. The group was going through a book called *Seeking Peace*. She had been underlining important points in the book and making side notes of personal applications. Pastor Kirsten explains that Cassie's brother, Chris, found the following note in her room on Tuesday night, when it became clear that she wouldn't be coming home. Cassie wrote this on the day she died:

"Now I have given up on everything else. I have found it to be the only way to really know Christ, and to experience the mighty power that brought Him back to life again, and to find out what it means to suffer and to die with Him. So, whatever it takes, I will be one who lives in the fresh newness of life of those who are alive with the dead."

Seventeen-year-old Crystal Woodman, a friend of Cassie's, says Cassie truly lived out her faith and was always finding ways to serve. She remembers how Cassie loved greeting first-time visitors to their youth group and how she enjoyed volunteering with an inner-city ministry called Victory Outreach.

Pastor Kirsten knows of Cassie's involvement with Victory Outreach, too. "She'd go down there along with the youth group and hang out with a pretty rough bunch," he says. "She'd talk to prostitutes, gang members and people just out of prison about the Lord. She was increasingly bold."

Crystal, who was one student spared from the bullets flying through Columbine's library, says, "Cassie loved photography and was really good at it. She liked to snowboard and hike and liked animals."

And above all else, Cassie cared about people. Crystal says Cassie had talked about her hopes to work in the medical field someday. "I know she was planning on volunteering at a hospital this summer," Crystal says. "And then she was going to cut off her hair for the chemo patients. It was amazing. She was constantly trying to help people."

With these few examples, it's easy to see that Cassie took on a sincere love for people since giving her life to Christ two years ago. "Cassie was a light for Christ," says seventeen-year-old Craig Moon, a close friend of Cassie's.

Crystal agrees. "She died for her faith. That's why she died and that's how she lived her whole life. She was a martyr for Jesus."

Cassie's parents, Brad and Misty Bernall, have this statement to share: "Our daughter, Cassie, was no saint. She was far from perfect, but she was prepared. Her final word, 'Yes,' will always be a challenge and inspiration to us. Our prayer is that her 'Yes' will be proclaimed aloud by many more to come. Cassie, as one of her friends expressed, has raised the bar for all of us. Let us be determined to see that it is never lowered."

Rachel Scott

Always taking opportunities to tell others about her faith in Christ, Rachel Scott often used her talents in the arts for God's glory. She acted in school plays and choreographed productions to Christian music for class assignments. One of her favorites was a mime to the Ray Boltz song "Watch the Lamb."

Rachel often expressed herself through poetry, too, and wrote one poem that illustrates the significance of each person knowing Jesus as Savior. Inside a print of her hand, Rachel wrote:

"What if you were to die today? What would happen to you? Where would you go? Tomorrow is not a promise, but a chance. It may not be there for you. After death, then what? Where will you spend your eternity? Will you have an eternal life without your loving Father, or will you be ripped from the arms of your Savior, Jesus Christ? Eternity is in your hands ... Change it!"

Rachel was near the end of her senior year of high school at the time of her death. She had dreamed of serving in Africa as a missionary. A coworker and friend of Rachel's, Rob Salyer, told *The Washington Post*, "I think Rachel thought of Africa because there's so much suffering there. She wanted to help relieve the suffering."

Student Sarah Arzola has a necklace with half a charm that says, "Best Friends for Life." "Rachel has the other one," Sarah said as she spoke with *The Denver Rocky Mountain News*. "We were complete opposites, but we were best friends."

Soon after Rachel's death, her mother, Beth Nimmo, spoke with a reporter from the Christian Broadcasting Network. She said, "I'm so glad Rachel knew the Lord. It is a comfort to know that our relationship will be restored at some point. She was everything a mother could want, and I thank God for letting me have her and letting me love and take care of her as long as I did."

The Good in the Bad

Because of the way Cassie and Rachel lived, much was accomplished in their death. The Holy Spirit worked through the testimonies of two young girls to change eternity for many other people. God has advanced his kingdom in a visible way through the tragedy in Littleton. As Joseph said in the Old Testament, "You intended to harm me, but God intended it for good to accomplish what is now being done, the saving of many lives" (Genesis 50:20).

"Cassie was ready," Crystal says. "We all have to be ready like Cassie was—constantly reading the Word, constantly serving, constantly living our lives for Christ."

* * *

The gunman cornered Cassie in the school library, pointed his gun in her face and screamed, "Do you believe in God?" Without hesitation, Cassie quickly responded, "YES! I believe!" And with that, she was killed.

I don't know if your friend will be cornered or persecuted for her faith, but the important thing is that she be ready—that we *all* be ready. I realize it's not easy for you to hear her talk about the possibility of dying as a martyr, but listen to her feelings and continue encouraging her to share them with you.

Since you're both Christians, why not pray regularly together? None of us knows how long we have left on this earth. Make it a point to ask God to continually keep you standing strong for him.

> This is how we know what love is: Jesus Christ laid down his life for us. And **we ought to lay down our lives** for our brothers.
>
> 1 JOHN 3:16, emphasis mine

Help!
I'm Stuck In My Comfort Zone!

Dear Susie:
   I've recently made a new friend, and she's really nice, but she doesn't know God. I don't know how to witness to her without sounding pushy.

Kellie

Unfortunately, many girls your age are so absorbed in their own struggles that they're unwilling or unable to reach out and minister to others. You're a bright exception, and I'm encouraged by your enthusiasm.

The Bible is very clear that Jesus wants *everyone* to be saved. "The Lord is not slow in keeping his promise, as some understand slowness. He is patient with you, not wanting anyone to perish, but everyone to come to repentance" (2 Peter 3:9).

It's comforting to know that Jesus wants your friend saved even more than you do! Love her unconditionally. Ask God to help you reflect his character. Talk about the Lord in a natural way—instead of preaching at her or "telling" her what she "should" know.

Have you ever given your personal testimony to someone? If not, now would be a great time to practice. Jot down what your life was like *before* you met Christ, how you came to know him in his fullness and the difference he's making in your life today. Try to keep it under three minutes.

Also, consider inviting her to your youth group. Surrounding her with several Christian friends from church will help her see the difference in your life and the lives of nonbelievers at school.

If you'd like more tips on witnessing, grab a copy of a book I wrote with a friend of mine: *Keeping Your Cool While Sharing Your Faith*.

How Can I Find a Best Friend?

Dear Susie:

I have many friends, but not one I can call a best friend. I don't know how long I can go without having a good Christian friend whom I can write to and talk with. Please help!

Megan

I'm glad you have several friends. A best friend is great, but not *essential* to your happiness. I'm guessing, from the sound of your letter, that you just don't have *Christian* friends. I admire you for wanting to establish a friendship with someone who shares your deepest belief in God.

Ask your mom to pray *with* you for God to raise up a Christian young lady at your school. It could be that there are several Christian students, but you're just not aware of it.

One way to find out who the Christians are is to participate at the annual "See You at the Pole" event every September. Christians all around the world meet at the flagpole of their schools on a specific day and pray for their school.

I'll give you the hotline number, so you can get more information, OK? (619-592-9200) Meanwhile, keep *being* a friend to those around you.

Do I Really Have to Be Friendly to Everyone?

Dear Susie:

I have a friend who's really tenderhearted. I mean, she'll see a crippled dog and start crying. And when someone new comes to school, she always tells me we should try to make friends with her. I don't know ... I'm just not that outgoing. But she keeps pushing me on this. Help!

Kimberly

Sounds like you're afraid to get out of your comfort zone. I admire your friend's willingness to befriend new students. It doesn't sound as if she's asking you to do this by yourself. Why couldn't you *together* reach out more to those around you?

There are definitely hundreds of lonely, hurting students right inside your school who could use a Christian influence and a smile.

I suggest you talk to God about it.

God Said ... I Said

This is a private conversation.
DON'T READ ... unless you enjoy eavesdropping.

God Said: What about Julianna?
I Said: What about her?
Why does she always eat lunch alone?
I don't know.
Have you ever thought about it?
Not really.
Why not?

Well, that's just her. I mean ... she *always* eats alone. I guess I'm just used to seeing her in the school cafeteria by herself.

Hmmm.

It's no big deal. She probably likes it.

Would *you* like it?

No way! I'm too much of a people-person to hang out by myself at lunchtime!

Yet you'd have to ... if no one chose to sit with you.

Whaddya mean if no one chose to sit with me? I've always got a *few* friends I can count on!

But what if you didn't?

C'mon, God. What are you getting at?

Think about it: What if you really *wanted* to be with people, but you couldn't find anyone to sit with you at lunch?

No one?

No one.

Well, that'd be pretty tough. I mean ... I ... I'd really be hurting inside. I'd probably go home and cry every day.

Good.

Good?!?

Good—now you're thinking outside of yourself.

Whaddya mean?

You're imagining how someone else might feel if she were all alone but didn't really want to be.

You mean ... Julianna?

Right.

Well, that's different. *She's* different.

How is she different?

Well, for one thing, she's always alone.

I thought we already covered this.

Well, what are you trying to say, God?

OK. Yes, she's alone. We've already established that fact. But *could* it be that she doesn't really *want* to be alone?

I don't know. I just always assumed she wanted it that way or she'd do something about it.

Hmmm. Remember when you first started riding the bus to school?

Yeah. That was third grade.

Right.

So?

You didn't know anyone on the bus. You sat with a different kid every day—hoping to make a friend—but everyone ignored you simply because you were the new "bus kid."

I forgot all about that. Man! That was really a hard year.

Yes, it was ... until February.

February?

It was February 3 that your older sister asked her friend Julie to consider *not* driving her little sister, Marcie, to school. She knew that you and Marcie were good friends and if Marcie would ride the bus with you, you'd be more comfortable.

Hey! I never knew Lindsey did that!

She loves you.

Lindsey asked Julie to encourage Marcie to ride my bus?

That's right. And since you only lived three blocks away from each other, Lindsey knew you'd both have the same route.

Wow. I'm really glad Lindsey did that, because Marcie and I had a great time on the bus! It felt soooo good to finally have a friend to ride with me—you know—someone to laugh with, talk with, *be* with.

Now back to Julianna.

Well, I don't ride the bus anymore.

I know. But the same principle is at work here.

You've lost me, God.

Think about it. You really *wanted* someone to sit with on the bus. But it never happened until someone else stepped in and helped you with the friendship you needed.

Yeah.

So never assume just because someone's alone that it's their choice. Maybe Julianna doesn't know *how* to do anything about it. If you needed help, maybe she could use some help, too.

OK, so what are you saying, God? Give it to me straight.

I want you to eat lunch with her.

You're kidding, right?

No. I was kidding when I gave the hyenas laughter. But I'm not kidding about Julianna needing a friend.

But what about *my* friends?

What about them?

I can't just leave them!

I didn't ask you to.

But you want me to eat lunch with Julianna! How can I just ignore my friends—the girls I eat with every single day—to go sit with a loner?

You don't have to leave them. Invite Julianna to eat at *your* table.

Oh, man!

Remember how hurt you were back in third grade?

Yeah.

Julianna's hurting, my child. I care about her. I need *you* to reach out to her.

But what'll I say?

Don't worry about that. I'll give you the words.

And what if she turns me down?

Don't worry about that, either. I've already started preparing her heart.

What do You mean?

Well ... she's been praying for a friend.

You're kidding?!!

No. That was the hyenas, remember?

Oh, yeah. But God ... you mean ... she's a Christian?

That's right. And she's been praying for three months that I'd help her find another Christian friend at this school.

Wow. I never knew.

I've been trying to speak to you.

You mean ... all that stuff my youth leader's been saying about bringing someone to church?

Yes.

And loving someone new?

Yes.

And those Sunday school lessons on not excluding others?

Yes.

And Mom asking me if I've made any new friends this year?

Yes.

Man! I sure am hardheaded sometimes. I'm sorry, Father. All

this time, I've been praying that you'd use me in a special way this year at school. And Julianna's been right under my nose the whole time! Why didn't I think of this on my own?

You were praying for an opportunity ... but you weren't looking for an opportunity. There's a difference.

Yeah! A big difference.

When you ask me to use you, always expect that I'll bring an opportunity your way to do just that.

Father, I *want* to be used.

I know, my child.

I *want* you to make a difference through me.

I will. But you've got to make the first move. YOU reach out ... and trust ME to do the rest.

Father, will you forgive me for being so blinded to the needs of those around me? I'm really sorry.

You're forgiven. And with a tender heart like that, I can use you in numerous ways this year.

Thanks, Father. I gotta go now.

Where are you going?

I'm gonna call Amber and Kelli and Emily and Kristine and remind them that you want to use us to make a difference in Julianna's life.

Great! I'll come with you.

Acknowledgments

"99 Reasons Why Going Solo Is A-OK" by Susie Shellenberger and Marty McCormack first appeared in the February 1999 issue of *Brio* magazine.

"Blessing in Disguise" by Becky Clemmons first appeared in the July 1998 issue of *Brio* magazine.

"Fighting the Food Phantom" by Laura Johnson as told to Tracy Pullen first appeared in the September 1992 issue of *Brio* magazine.

"From Gothic to Godly" by Susie Shellenberger first appeared in the February 1999 issue of *Brio* magazine.

"Hey, World! Here I Am!" by Marty McCormack first appeared in the September 1998 issue of *Brio* magazine.

"Remembering Columbine" by Marty McCormack first appeared in the September 1999 issue of *Brio* magazine.

"This Could Happen to You" by Helen Walden and Sharon Sipos first appeared in the January 1999 issue of *Brio* magazine.

"Who, Me—a Mooch?" by Anne Williman first appeared in the June 1999 issue of *Brio* magazine.

"You've Got What it Takes" by Marty McCormack first appeared in the September 1999 issue of *Brio* magazine.

About the Author

Susie travels worldwide as a youth and women's speaker and also co-hosts Focus on the Family's weekly national radio talk show for teens, "Life on the Edge: Live!" Contact your Christian radio station for more information, or call 1-800-232-6459 to find out if it's on in your area. To request a complimentary copy of *Brio* magazine, you can call the above number as well.